Learning at Work

D1264158

Copyright © 2005 The President and Fellows of Harvard College. All rights reserved.

Published by Project Zero, Harvard Graduate School of Education, Cambridge MA.

No part of this publication may be reproduced, stored in a retrieval system or transmitted in any form or by any means, electronic, mechanical, photocopying, recording, scanning, or otherwise, except as permitted under Section 107 of 108 of the 1976 United States Copyright Act, without either the prior written permission of the Publisher, or authorization through payment of the appropriate per-copy fee to the Copyright Clearance Center, Inc., 222 Rosewood Drive, Danvers, MA 01923, 978-750-8400, or on the web as www.copyright.com. Requests to the Publisher for permission should be addressed to the Publications Department, Project Zero, Harvard Graduate School of Education, 124 Mt. Auburn Street, Cambridge, MA 02138, 617-495-4342.

Limit of Liability/Disclaimer of Warranty: While the publisher and authors have used their best efforts in preparing this book, they make no representations of warranties with respect to the accuracy of completeness of the contexts of this book and specifically disclaim any implied warranties of merchantability or fitness of a particular purpose. No warranty may be created or extended by sales representative or written sales materials. The advice and strategies contained herein may not be suitable for your situation. You should consult with a professional where appropriate. Neither the publisher nor authors shall be liable for any loss of profit or any other commercial damages, including but not limited to special incidental, consequential, or other damages.

ISBN 0-9725705-1-9

Printed in the United States of America

CONTENTS

AUTHORS

Daniel Wilson is a researcher at Harvard Graduate School of Education's Project Zero. He has worked closely with teachers, schools and businesses in North and South America to improve teaching and learning practices. He was a lead researcher and the project manager for the "Understanding for Organizations" project while living in Bogotá, Colombia. He currently oversees the Harvard Graduate School of Education's "Learning Innovations Laboratory" with David Perkins.

David Perkins is Professor of Education at the Harvard Graduate School of Education as well as a founding member and leader of Harvard Project Zero, a research and development group at the School of Education. He has published widely on the themes of thinking, understanding, and learning. David was a co-principal investigator on the "Understanding for Organizations" project.

Dora Bonnet is a researcher and trainer of managers at the Universidad Jorge Tadeo Lozano in Bogotá, Colombia. She has been coordinator and head of English departments in several schools and universities in Bogotá, and worked on the development of reading materials for non-native university students in a joint project between the Universidad de los Andes and the British Council in Bogotá. She was a lead researcher and coordinator of the Understanding for Organizations Project for Colombia.

Cecilia Miani is an anthropologist and Harvard M.Ed. She has been an anthropology professor and academic administrator at the Universidad de los Andes in Bogotá, Colombia. She started the program "Opción Colombia" which supports university students to work with needy and marginal communities in various Latin-American countries. She was a lead researcher in the "Understanding for Organizations" project in Colombia.

Chris Unger was a Principal Investigator and Research Associate at Project Zero of the Harvard Graduate School of Education for several years, and was co-principal investigator of the "Understanding for Organizations" project with David Perkins. He has worked with hundreds of teachers and dozens of schools and non-profit and for-profit organizations in North and South America. He continues to work with schools in an effort to transform schooling practices and structures so that meaningful engagement, passion, and the pursuit of the generative life is at the heart of our work and learning.

ACKNOWLEDGEMENTS

This book reports a cross-cultural collaboration between scholars, managers, and researchers from La Universidad de Bogotá Jorge Tadeo Lozano (informally known as "La Tadeo") in Bogotá, Colombia and Harvard Graduate School of Education's Project Zero. The project would not have been possible without the vigilant support and pioneering vision of the leaders at La Tadeo. The authors wish to thank Evaristo Obregon (Rector during the project) and Fanny Mestre (Vice Rector of Finances and Administration), who devoted funding, time and spirit to the "Understanding for Organizations" project.

This project had many levels of integral players who were vital in its development. The authors would like to thank Veronica Boix-Mansilla of Project Zero, who participated as a researcher on the project and insightfully advised throughout. Carlos Eduardo Vasco, Colombian educator and visiting scholar at Project Zero, also graciously participated in conversations that supported the concepts in this book. At La Tadeo, we wish to thank Miguel Bermudez whose original pedagogical dream brought Project Zero to that university. Special thanks also goes to La Tadeo manager Juan Sastoque who maintained interest, kept morale high and limitlessly supported the learning of his colleagues throughout the organization. The authors are also grateful to the facilitators, Ramón Carrillo, Guillermo Forero, Luis Eduardo Mantilla, and Jaime Melo who enthusiastically participated as project researchers, model managers, developers of materials, and leaders for small groups of managers in inquiry.

We are indebted to the dozens of La Tadeo managers who shared their time in meetings, opened their offices and put into practice the ideas illustrated throughout this book. Specifically, we are grateful to La Tadeo managers Judy Avellaneda, Jesus Balcazar, Carlos Morales, Yolanda Rugeles, Bibiana Valenzuela, and Marvin Viloria all of whom invited researchers to work closely with them and their offices. The support of Alberto Cardona was also instrumental, keeping the project on focus and on time. These and many other insightful La Tadeo managers were invaluable in crafting an understanding approach to organizational change at La Tadeo.

The logistics of this project depended greatly on the expert office coordination by Lisa Frontado and Dorothy MacGillivray at Project Zero, and Sandra Milena Ortiz, Rosalba Gutierrez and Dilsa Jimenez at La Tadeo. We also extend a special thanks to Luis Augusto Ortegón, Luis Francisco Alvarado and Ricardo Ladino for organizing and coordinating the logistical aspects of the many weekly project meetings and workshops at the University.

As a final note, the authors extend continued gratitude to the forward thinking Rosario Jaramillo for her initial interest in fueling collaborations between Project Zero and Colombia. Her wisdom and unending energies remain an inspiration to us all.

FOREWORD

Organizational Weather

Organizations have weather. They have sunny days and stormy days. They have rainy seasons and dry ones. They have climates serene or tumultuous. Moreover, just as the real weather is always with us, so is organizational weather—because we live out our lives in organizational contexts large and small. The workplace, the family, clubs, schools, universities, all are organizations, and for all of them the organizational weather makes a great difference in how and whether we thrive.

Like the real weather, organizational weather can change. It can change through shifts in leadership, when a new overall or departmental leader brings in fresh philosophies and commitments. It can change through market trends that make what the organization does more or less valued. It can change through slow demographic shifts in age, gender, and other characteristics of those who make up the organization. It can even change through deliberate effort, the analog of seeding clouds to make rain to help the crops to grow.

This latter path—changing organizational weather deliberately—is one of the most attractive but also one of the hardest. Like the real weather, organizational weather is a systems phenomenon, a consequence of myriad factors that yield emergent effects, and thus difficult to direct. However, the quest is a worthy one, because people rarely live in a supportive and generative organizational climate. Too often it is too chaotic, too autocratic, or too egocentric to provide for the thriving life that people individually and collectively deserve.

Like everyone else, both authors of this foreword have lived most of their lives within various organizations. Indeed, the first author served as Rector of the Universidad Jorge Tadeo Lozano throughout the period of the initiative reported in this book, during which time he sought to generate good organizational weather.

One of these diverse endeavors was the launching of the Understanding for Organizations initiative reported in this book, affectionately known as UfO because sometimes changes in the organizational weather seem about as evasive as UfOs do. The pages to come tell the story of its methods, its data, its discovery, its difficulties, and its results. Although the story of a particular case, the Understanding for Organizations initiative concerns organizational weather everywhere. It brings forward fundamental considerations about how people can work thoughtfully, creatively, and happily—or less so—depending on collective structures and practices. This book speaks to anyone who would like better organizational weather. We hope that it and other contributions like it will lead a good many people toward sunnier organizational days.

Evaristo Obregon, *Bogotá, Colombia*
David Perkins, *Cambridge, Massachusetts*

Learning at Work

1. UNDERSTANDING IN ACTION

An Expedition to the Chemistry Department

It was early spring when Luis Alvarez*, an administrator at La Universidad de Bogotá Jorge Tadeo Lozano in Colombia, went over to the department of chemistry and posed a question to a professor. He asked, "What would you really like your teaching laboratories to be like?" So obvious was the question, it might seem amazing that it had not been asked before. But that wasn't the way things usually worked at "La Tadeo" (which everyone called the university for short). Administration was administration; the academic area was the academic area. To be sure, they had something to do with one another. But they didn't actually *talk* that much.

This time, they did talk. The manager sought and valued the interests, concerns, and needs of the professors, while the professors also learned something of the budgetary limitations the context imposed. They explored issues of equipment, physical environment, and training. Luis Alvarez developed a plan and budget for a number of improvements for presentation to his boss. For the first time ever, the plan and budget were approved without changes. New and better equipment resulted, along with a training course for its use.

---

* For this and later stories which appear, the names of people and some circumstances have been changed to preserve the individuals' privacy.

A Commitment to Understanding

Why did Luis Alvarez break precedent and walk over to the chemistry department? He was trying to understand something. He sought to understand what was really needed by faculty for the best teaching. Why did he seek such an understanding at that moment? Because in that spring, understanding was in the air at La Tadeo. The flag of understanding was being raised to guide the organizational development.

The story began much earlier and in a different part of the university. Two years before, Miguel Bermudez, a vice-rector of the university and head of the postgraduate programs, attended an institute at the Harvard Graduate School of Education conducted by a research and development group called Harvard Project Zero.* Rosario Jaramillo, a Colombian who had been a visiting scholar at the Harvard Graduate School of Education, had alerted him to their work. Project Zero, founded in 1967, has developed a number of models of intelligence, thinking, creativity, understanding, and learning that have informed educational practices from childhood through adulthood across a range of subject areas and out-of-school contexts.

One emphasis of the summer institute at Project Zero was a teaching methodology called Teaching for Understanding. Rosario Jaramillo had worked on the team developing this pedagogical framework. It foregrounded active learning in a systematic way that allowed individual teachers ample room to express their own styles. Miguel Bermudez liked what he saw. Moreover, his postgraduate programs had a tradition of striving to improve instruction. So he invited researchers from Project Zero along with Colombian collaborators

---

* An endnotes section at the end of this book describes more about Project Zero and houses references and further information as ideas are introduced throughout the book.

2

to design and carry out a program of teacher development for the professors in the post-graduate programs at La Tadeo.

The program proceeded well and indeed continues as these words are written. But more than that happened. La Tadeo Rector Evaristo Obregon participated seriously in the initial Teaching for Understanding workshops in Bogotá. (Rector of a university in Colombia is equivalent to president of a university in the United States.) He liked what he saw too. In addition, he knew that organizational development initiatives already underway at La Tadeo could benefit from a framework that focused on learning. With a leap of the imagination, he tendered a remarkable invitation to the team from Project Zero. "Work with us," he said, "to transform this model of teaching and learning into a model of organizational development. Make it something not just for teaching. Focus on the core administration—the business people here, the ones that handle billing, purchasing, physical plant, construction planning."

The Rector's invitation was a striking opportunity to translate ideas born from basic studies of human learning into the field of organizational learning. Within a few months, a team of collaborators from La Tadeo and Project Zero began to design a program called Understanding for Organizations. Just a few months after that, Luis Alvarez was building his own understanding by having conversations with chemistry professors.

A History of Expeditions

This was an unusual step for the administration of a university. Innumerable corporations have undertaken programs to streamline operations, cultivate creativity, advance productivity, and improve quality. However, in universities, conspicuous innovation usually takes the form of professors' professional research. Structural innovation usually occurs through new academic

3

programs and approaches to teaching, as with the Teaching for Understanding initiative in the postgraduate programs. La Tadeo was different. Here, the technical administration cast themselves in the role of experimenters and innovators.

Indeed, an expeditionary spirit lay deep in the history of La Universidad de Bogotá Jorge Tadeo Lozano. The university was founded in celebration of the cultural and scientific work initiated by the Colombian Botanical expedition during the latter part of the eighteenth century. This expedition was the first scientific mission sponsored by Spain to investigate the natural history of Colombia and search for new economic opportunities in the colonies. Jose Celestino Mutis, a Spanish priest and doctor of great learning and insight, directed the expedition. Among his co-workers were some highly respected intellectuals such as Francisco Jose de Caldas and Jorge Tadeo Lozano.

The Enlightenment provided the intellectual context of the Botanical Expedition, summarized in three words: progress, tolerance and freedom. This movement also reinforced the use of reason, science, and mathematics to understand the world and its social and physical realities. In Colombia the Botanical expedition had scientific, political, economic and social influence. Besides scholarly outcomes, the expedition discovered quinine, which later saw extensive use in medicine. The Botanical Expedition was the first intercultural and academic work of importance done in Colombia and a landmark in defining Colombia's potential. In remembrance, La Universidad de Bogotá Jorge Tadeo Lozano was formed in its spirit in 1954.

For decades after, La Tadeo ambled along as a medium sized institution where a sound education could be obtained. But new leadership and sharp financial management in the early 1990's lead to an era of dramatic improvement and expansion that expressed the vital energy of the Botanical Expedition. Growing pains were an inevitable accompaniment. The administration's structure came to reflect the unplanned growth of the institution. New offices were added without eliminating old ones or fusing them with those that did part of the same task. For example, the postgraduate school, which appeared late in the story of the University, depended on the central financial area for its administration. The central office often had different ideas about the way money should be handled. As the organization grew, the administration assumed a pyramidal structure where deeply marked hierarchies hindered the flow of information, concentrating almost all the decisions at the top. Interoffice communication and collaboration was limited, each office an island attending to and sometimes defending its own territory.

Many employees in La Tadeo recognized these challenges and steps were taken to address them. A series of meetings identified redundant processes, contradictory policies, and communication breakdowns. All this was gathered in a document called the Blue Book. Some improvements were introduced, although much remained to be done. It was at this point the Rector invited Project Zero to join them in a search for new pedagogical approaches to organizational development. The Understanding for Organizations initiative was seen as one among other ways of advancing the spirit of inquiry and change begun with the Blue Book.

This history of innovation at La Tadeo established the climate for the present initiative. Throughout the process to the present moment, Evaristo Obregon and Vice-Rector for management and finances Fanny Mestre have sustained a robust political will for change, providing financial and people resources and declaring it an officially approved part of administrators' roles to attend frequent meetings and commit time to the process of change.

Understanding in Action

Why *understanding* for organizations? Terms like understanding and organizational development do not so often occur in the same sentence. The word understanding more brings to mind the challenges of high school algebra or the playfully enigmatic writings of Borges or the personal empathy of good human relations than organizational development. The world of organizational change instead conjures up ideas like reengineering, total quality management, or scenario building. Understanding aside, even the somewhat less ambitious phrase "organizational learning" sometimes seems like an oxymoron. How could an approach to organizational development find a foundation in the idea of understanding?

An answer came from a particular view of understanding developed by the educational researchers at Project Zero. In everyday language, understanding often has a rather static character. People attain understanding by "grasping" an idea or "apprehending" it—taking possession of it and owning it in some sense. In the same spirit, people often speak of "catching on" to something and aver, "You either get it or you don't." This sense of understanding can be traced back to the very structure of its Latin root *comprehendere*, with *prehendere* meaning to grasp. Even scientific writings on understanding often treat it as a matter of possessing the right thing—a good schema or mental model of the concept in question.

The notion of understanding advocated by the Project Zero group had a much more dynamic character. Understanding was treated as a matter of action, even for academic concepts. Understanding Newton's laws meant much more than just having the right mental model in mind. It meant being able to put Newton's laws into action by making predictions, explaining situations, designing gadgets, comparing and contrasting with other laws, and the like. In general, understanding anything was a matter of being able to think and act flexibly with what you know. In keeping with this action-oriented notion of understanding, acquiring understanding was less like "catching on" and more like developing a flexible performance through practice and reflection.

This dynamic conception of understanding suited the world of organizations as well as it suited professors and classrooms, hence Understanding for Organizations. Managers may read a book about project management or good communications practices and follow its ideas and arguments well enough. However, true understanding of practical ideas goes beyond intellectual understanding. It means bringing the ideas into the flow of work, where it really counts. It means using those ideas creatively, intelligently, and resourcefully day by day. Luis Alvarez's understanding of laboratory needs was not a matter of having the right abstract theory of the design of teaching laboratories. It was a matter of thinking about the needs, speaking to professors, weaving together considerations of equipment cost, physical layout, scheduling, and more, to evolve actions that made sense. He did not understand and then act, but built his understanding through intentional action.

The same held for other administrators at La Tadeo. Understanding leadership was not a matter of knowing a few principles and then following them. It was a matter of acting thoughtfully in real situations. Understanding how a group could collaborate better was not a matter of knowing the five most important tricks of collaborative work. It was a matter of doing—making good moves in real situations that built strong relationships and moved the work along. Understanding was nothing abstract and static. It was understanding in action.

La Tadeo managers explored this active conception of understanding by first coming to know the Teaching for Understanding model used in the postgraduate programs of La Tadeo. Besides the idea of understanding in action, the framework emphasized the importance of understanding goals: What was one trying to understand—about laboratories, about leadership, about effective meetings? The framework emphasized broad themes called generative topics and throughlines that could inform many facets of organizational life. One such, for example, was the leader as a teacher. Another was care—care of others, care for the institution, care of the community. These and other throughlines will be explored in later chapters.

A final facet of the framework concerned evaluation. The process of building understanding-in-action called not just for evaluation at the end but continuous self-monitoring, feedback and redirection along the way. How did Luis Alvarez feel he was doing on the laboratory project so far? Had he talked to the important people? Did he have a clear vision of the financial implications? What big puzzles remained? Questions such as these were symptoms of understanding-in-the-making. They were signs of the kind of ongoing assessment so important to the cultivation of understanding in action.

This initial framework underwent considerable transformation during the initiative at La Tadeo. But the central theme of understanding in action and the core concepts of the framework survived various changes of vocabulary and framing to continue to inform innovation at La Universidad Jorge Tadeo Lozano.

Understanding in action provided the umbrella concept for the innovations at La Tadeo. Beyond that, four themes help to organize the account, coming together in various combinations throughout this book. The themes are: bridging the idea-action gap, culture makers, integrating work and learning, and structural supports. The rest of this chapter introduces these themes and previews the chapters to come.

Theme 1: Bridging the Idea-Action Gap

Both common experience and a considerable literature on organizational change suggest that the key challenge of organizational change in general could be stated in three words: the *idea-action gap*. Change, especially lasting change, comes hard. Wonderful ideas lie at the beginning— ideas about more humane and efficient organizations, improvement of quality, superior communications, increased creativity and productivity, skillful collaboration. Many of these are effective ideas in a particular sense: When carefully put into action, they yield real gains in people's well-being and the productivity of the organization. However, most of the time, the ideas do not make it into action. There is a huge gap between good ideas and consequent actions in the world.

Inevitably, the idea-action gap was part of the challenge at La Tadeo. Not all participants were like Luis Alvarez. For instance, Flora Ramirez was a fairly regular attendee in the small meetings to advance various causes within the administration. She reflected energetically on the various problems around the university and offered her own interpretations about why this or that had happened. She participated in the conversation by commenting on others' work. But Flora never managed to get much done outside the meetings.

She was in a good position to act, being in charge of an office involving several other personnel. She had sensible ideas when it came time to propose initiatives. However, they would get lost in the course of the busy weeks. An urgent issue in her office would sweep other plans aside for days on end. She would report feeling hesitant and holding back because of how she thought her office staff or her boss might react. Now and again, Flora would follow through on something. Still, compared to the best participants, Flora wasn't accomplishing much beyond being a good meeting participant.

Anyone who has ever participated in initiatives of organizational development will recognize Flora. Indeed, there are many Floras. In some organizational change initiatives, most people play the role of Flora—or worse. At least Flora was interested. Sometimes people become desultory participants or, worse, downright resisters and antagonists.

This should not come as a surprise. It happens in personal life as much as in organizational life. We strive to eat and smoke less, align our behavior with the Ten Commandments, and generally try to live up to our ideal selves on various fronts. Sometimes we succeed, but often we fail. Likewise, in the world of organizations, in the office next to yours or down the hall, there are Floras. There are people willing enough to engage ideas, sometimes positively, sometimes skeptically. But, one way or another, not much real change occurs.

From the standpoint of the initiative at La Tadeo, how should we understand the idea-action gap, and what can be done about it?

Buried Belief Systems

One force behind the idea-action gap is the inarticulate beliefs people hold that drive their actions. Chris Argyris and Donald Schön write about the contrast between *espoused theories* and *theories-in-use*. For example, a manager may espouse democratic leadership practices quite sincerely, yet behave in an autocratic way without even recognizing it. Argyris and Schön suggest that such a manager at some level holds a less democratic theory of leadership that surfaces in behavior. In a similar spirit, organizational theorist Edgar Schein discusses how entrenched and unrecognized belief systems shape behavior in organizations. When change initiatives challenge these belief systems, the result is often a backlash from what Schein terms the *organizational immune system*. Kets de Vries offers another perspective along the same lines. Adopting a Freudian metaphor, he posits a kind of organizational unconscious where conflicts, tensions, anxieties, and defensive patterns lurk beneath the surface and drive overt behavior in ways not apparent to the participants.

This could be a problem for Flora. Her innovative ideas might run aground on the rocks of workplace habits that reflect beliefs of which she is not very aware. There are many ways to approach such difficulties. One common pattern might be called the *therapeutic model,* in analogy to a style of clinical therapy. The general idea is to bring to the surface through open discussion the unrecognized mental models driving behavior. This typically means a facilitator working with people one-on-one or in a small group to expose hidden belief systems relevant to managerial style. Such probing can sometimes lead to revisions of belief and important changes in behavior. On the other hand, sometimes people persist in previous beliefs even after recognizing them, or adopt compromises that do not lead to much change in behavior.

Silent Caution

Although unrecognized beliefs may be part of the story, it's also important to consider silent caution. When people quietly resist a change, they often seem to be quite aware of what they are doing. Flora, for instance, may feel that, by participating actively in the conversation but not doing much, she is protecting her status in the organization by "not rocking the boat." Or she may see herself as avoiding yet another fad that probably will blow over in a few months. There is no subtle mystery about it. Although Flora would be unlikely to admit motives such as these in a meeting, she might well share her doubts in a corridor conversation with a colleague. Moreover, in many situations, motives of this sort are entirely reasonable. The threats and faddishness may be all too real.

Practical Barriers to Action

Buried and unvoiced beliefs aside, the path from idea to action still is not an easy one. Flora may be quite genuinely committed to more efficient and democratic collaboration, and yet not know what moves to make to cultivate it. Flora may harbor old habits that sabotage her sincere efforts toward better collaboration. On a more mundane level, Flora may discover that it's hard to introduce new and genuinely desired practices into her own behavior—not to mention others' behavior—because everyone is simply so very busy.

Cultural Barriers to Action

Any organization, and even individual offices, has a culture. Implicit values and expectations, habitual patterns of interaction that make up "the way things are done," characteristic risks and rewards for various kinds of behavior, and similar features make up this culture. Flora may start out with the best intentions, but run into cultural roadblocks. She may discover that the people in her offices are comfortable in their routines and not eager to experiment. Her efforts may lead to disruptions of routine—common during innovation—that have a temporary negative impact on performance. She may conclude that it's not safe to try a new direction. Or if it's safe to try, it may not be safe to fail.

How to Bridge the Idea-Action Gap

With challenges such as the foregoing in mind, the team at La Tadeo sought to learn more about the idea-action gap and find ways to bridge it, or even close it so that idea and action became seamless. In broadest terms, the approach was to foreground not just reflective examination of beliefs but intelligent action in the world. The team sought to foster an awareness of the organizational culture, the ways in which it supported or discouraged innovation, and how to cope with barriers.

12

However, the team had to get beyond the idea that helping the administrators to reflect and arrive at insights would automatically provoke innovation. Participants in such initiatives can easily arrive at a range of insights without doing much to change anything!

Accordingly, action environments and expectations were essential factors in getting beyond reflection. It was important to encourage intelligent exploratory practical action, backed up by reflection and by informative and non-threatening sources of feedback. It was important to give participants good reason to try out new practices, whether they believed in them or not. The team sought to make it safe, frame it as experimental, provide social support, foster ideals, and sustain a coherent and consistent philosophy and framework that defended against scatter. It was equally important to make calculated efforts to manage negative forces, by, for instance, mediating conflicts and encouraging people not to expect miracles overnight.

However, all such efforts would have been fruitless without help from the top. A key component in any such initiative is top managers as public supporters and models. The team sought frequent public support and (within practical limits) active participation of people high in the organization. Without their signals that real change is a priority, little was likely to happen.

Finally, action-friendly frameworks and tools played a central role. Such frameworks and tools were needed to support the cognitive demands of the process, to help people think about what they were doing before, during, and after action. Concepts and strategies that are complicated, cumbersome, and hard to remember are not likely to penetrate the continuous momentum of managers' busy days.

Strategies such as these foster understanding in action. When this works at its best, new beliefs and a new repertoire of actions develop together in a natural way. Because the emphasis falls on understanding in action, one might speak of a performance model of change. This conception of change may not help with all the Floras of the world. Indeed, it's worth recalling that some of them have good reason to hang back. But it helped with many at La Tadeo.

Theme 2: Culture Makers

Luis Alvarez and Flora Ramirez are individuals. Their successes and difficulties illustrate the various forces that make it easier or harder for individuals to act in new ways in an organizational setting. However, organizational transformation involves much more than cultivating growth person by person. An organizational perspective is needed. In fact, one might say that, fundamentally, the kinds of changes envisioned here call for developing a culture of learning.

What does this mean in concrete terms? First of all, it means adopting a multilayered perspective that recognizes the involvement of individuals, groups, and the whole organization. Individuals participate through interacting with others pairwise, in groups, and as part of the organizational collective. Groups in turn—teams, offices, committees, and the like—typically have their own microcultures influenced by but also somewhat independent of the organization around them. Finally, some values and practices pervade the organization as a whole.

At these levels, a culture of learning entails continuous openness to learning through action, feedback, and reflection. A culture of learning means that it is reasonably safe to try new things, and reasonably safe to fail and learn from mistakes. Such attitudes and practices cannot be taken for granted. As already discussed, patterns of defensiveness and other forces of resistance stand in the way of a culture of learning. Furthermore, trying to deal with such barriers only at the individual level would certainly fail. Luis, Flora, and their colleagues would not find support within the organization as a whole or the various microcultures in which they participate. Accordingly, it was important in this initiative to deal directly with attitudes and practices at the social level, by working with various offices and the university administration as a whole.

Ideals as Culture Makers

At any level, ideals are an important force in developing new attitudes and behaviors. Luis's ideals of collaboration and commitment foster a culture of learning, while Flora's marginal participation sends opposing messages. The initiative at La Tadeo emphasized such ideals as collaboration, commitment, care, and generativity. In the various meetings and other collective activities, we explicitly discussed and celebrated ideals that looked toward what might be called a *generative organization*, where individuals, groups, and the entire organization grew and thrived.

Leaders as Culture Makers

Experiences at La Tadeo made plain how important leaders were in the making and remaking of a culture, from individual office managers to the Rector and Vice-Rectors. The words and actions of authority figures set expectations for others under their direction and for those who come in contact with them. The policies they announce, whether coherent or scattered, the styles they adopt, whether democratic or autocratic, the way they handle information, whether with secrecy or openness, all shape culture. How safe it was for subordinates to share thoughts frankly with a leader, and whether doing so actually made any difference in courses of action taken were key factors in microcultures. As noted earlier, top management plays a special role here. Continued explicit and public support, official allocation of time, and role modeling are essential for such projects.

Accordingly, it was important to work through the leadership of La Tadeo at all levels. We could not always generate the interest and commitment from particular managers that one might like. But often we could, even from time to time inspiring a Flora to fuller participation.

Tools as Culture Makers

Certainly tools like the flint knife and the stone axe helped to make early hunter-gatherer cultures what they were. Interestingly, conceptual tools are just as important in shaping a culture. Progress toward a culture of learning at La Tadeo required introducing conceptual tools that participants carried around in their minds as guides for new patterns of thought and action. A number of these tools appear in the following chapters. They address everything from ways of giving feedback to principles of conduct for leaders in establishing a positive culture.

Culture-making is not an easy enterprise. It involves a myriad of considerations and a multitude of tactics. The development team can hardly claim to have achieved anything like an ideal culture of learning within the administration of La Tadeo. But at least serious steps have been taken in that direction, with substantial positive consequences.

Actions as Culture Makers

We usually think of actions as reflecting culture—including the culture of an office or organization. But the opposite is just as true: Actions that others see *make* culture. Actions and interactions that reflect the status quo make culture in the sense of reaffirming and sustaining the dominant culture. Those that run contrary to norms have the potential of redirecting culture if they take hold. When a group takes the time to think something through, when a manager handles feedback to a subordinate sensitively, emphasizing positive points as well as concerns, when an executive reconsiders a decision already made in the light of legitimate concerns raised by others, these send powerful messages to everyone around that thoughtful, creative, and learning-oriented behavior is appropriate. They, as well as actions that cut in the opposite direction, constitute what we will later call *symbolic conduct*, the symbolic side of actions that goes beyond the immediate practical occasion. From this perspective, participants in an organization—and especially those in a leadership role—have a responsibility to consider how their actions make culture and what kind of a culture they are making.

Theme 3: Integrating Work and Learning

Organizational learning is a popular and important theme in contemporary writings on organizations. It is important that individuals within organizations learn well, to advance their personal understanding and skill as well as to advance the interests of the organization. Also, teams, divisions, and even the whole organization can be said to learn, for instance through acquiring new organizational routines or through establishing new systems of tacit beliefs that shape the organizational culture. Peter Senge offers another account of what might be learned. Widely known for his writings on organizational learning, Senge identifies five "disciplines" important to the learning organization, including personal mastery, mental models, building shared vision, team learning, and the fifth and integrative discipline, systems thinking.

Integrating work and learning names our particular perspective on organizational learning. In many organizational settings, attention to learning occurs off-site or at least out of the normal workflow, in workshops, seminars, and the like. Although such mechanisms can make a significant contribution, they tend to suffer from the idea-action gap. People acquire skills and understandings out of the work flow and have difficulty

17

translating them into authentic practice. Another typical problem of out-of-workflow learning concerns time allocations. In most settings, this amounts to a very few days a year, not much to support significant professional development of individuals, groups, or a whole organization.

In contrast, *integrating work and learning* concerns a range of practices that occur during the workflow. Ordinary activities can adopt forms and structures that favor learning rather than the execution of entrenched routines. Also, members of an organization can undertake inquiry projects that accomplish immediate practical ends and build understanding within the organization.

One useful way to think about integrating work and learning recognizes a rough distinction between different *time zones* of learning as we have sometimes called them: learning in the moment, learning day by day, and learning long-term.

Learning in the Moment

Organizational life is full of momentary interactions of various kinds—an exchange of feedback, a moment of mutual planning or decision making, issuing or receiving commands, and so on. Such interactions can follow patterns that foster learning or patterns that work against learning and reinforce entrenched routines. Feedback, for example, can take forms that provoke defensiveness and sour relationships or forms that cultivate individual and group development and strengthen relationships. Leaders can issue commands gracefully or in autocratic ways that alienate people. Commands can be overspecific, or so vague that people become confused, or ideally can leave the right amount of room for people to take responsibility, make their own way with the task, and learn from it.

The moment-to-moment flow of work is an efficient setting to cultivate learning, since the work needs to be done in any case. The chapters to come introduce concepts and tools that make interactions more oriented to learning.

Learning Day by Day

Besides momentary interactions, organizational life includes many larger-scale events: meetings and series of meetings, team activities, projects, and so on. These too present opportunities for learning. They are settings for learning in the moment but also their overall conduct can foster or undermine learning over longer cycles of time. Leadership roles have great importance here, because managers and other leaders are the figures that most influence the organization of larger-scale activities. As emphasized earlier under leaders as culture makers, their behavior presents models that others tend to emulate, for better or worse. Beyond modeling, a leader may conduct meetings in ways more open and inquiring or less so. A leader may engage people in organizing a series of tasks or organize the set of tasks for them.

Besides individual leaders, teams and other groups can conduct themselves in more or less open, exploratory, and inquiry-oriented ways. The following chapters present a variety of frameworks and strategies for supporting learning-oriented meetings and projects.

Learning Long-Term

Most organizations undertake occasional programs of improvement and innovation. The people conducting such initiatives can approach them in ways that emphasize learning—inquiry, exploration, and loops of evaluation and refinement—or in styles that stress straightforward cookie-cutter implementation. Courses, series of workshops, and other such events that remove learners from the workflow can take pains to cultivate transfer back into the workflow and to follow-up with participants to support and encourage their progress.

Beyond particular innovations and courses, large-scale projects such as the Understanding for Action initiative can adopt strategies that emphasize impact on the actual patterns of work in the organization rather than just cerebral learning.

The chapters to come offer a general methodology for improvement and innovation within an organization, one that integrates long-term learning with practical improvements in its work.

Theme 4: Structural Supports

Since interactions, roles, and initiatives of improvement and innovation present abundant opportunities for learning, one might expect to find that most organizations are learning organizations. Yet experience teaches us just the opposite: Most organizations get stuck in old patterns. Why is this?

Inevitably, several forces work against attention to learning. Many people within organizations see work as a matter of doing what people already know how to do well, rather than as a process of inquiry and learning. Entrenchment of routines and social forces against "rocking the boat" allow alienating and inefficient practices to persist. The tendency to think of learning as occurring primarily out of the workflow makes learning seem costly.

The shifts of attitude called for require more than putting new ideas on the table and arguing persuasively for them. Integrating work and learning demands structural supports within an organization—official policies, established customs, printed guidelines, strategies on handy cards, physical settings, staff dedicated to the mission—anything that remains a salient presence as people come and go. This is no less so of the first two themes, bridging the idea-action gap and culture makers. Recall that buried belief systems, unvoiced skepticism, and practical and cultural barriers to action maintained the idea-action gap. We suggested plans to bridge the idea-action gap. However, such plans evaporate over time without structural supports. We noted the power of culture makers such as ideals, leaders, tools, and actions to create a culture of learning. However, these culture makers themselves need structural supports to maintain their presence in the complex and shifting environment of organizations.

What forms might those structural supports take? One of the most important is policies that commit time for thinking, learning, and practical action to improve the organization and the well-being of the people in it. The kind of time needed differs from release days for workshops. Rather, policies need to sanction time for frequent brief small-group meetings where people can advance skills of feedback, facilitation, and the like that immediately become woven into the workflow. People need time for initiatives of improvement and innovation carried out in ways that emphasize inquiry. In addition, policies or customs that support specific learning-oriented practices can help, for instance, a custom of someone facilitating meetings rather than just letting them flow, and a custom of rotating facilitation so that people gain skills.

Policies and customs aside, strategies benefit from physical supports. Written guidelines can help with complex strategies. Simple forms to fill out aid in tracking innovations through their various phases. Tips printed on small cards can support the facilitation of meetings.

Physical and social setting also has importance. For instance, balanced collaborative conversations typically occur better at round or square tables than long boardroom tables. Staff with a specific commitment to foster development can make a huge difference through persistent efforts. Neither the general spirit of under-standing for organizations nor specific practices for bridging the idea-action gap, making cultures, or integrating work and learning are likely to thrive without the support of policies, customs, physical supports, and appropriate physical and social environments.

Continuing the Journey

What then are some of the details? How did this initiative begin, where has it gone, and with what results? By way of a preview:

Chapter 2, Cultivating Consciousness, relates the first steps of the intervention at La Tadeo. It emphasizes the importance of key questions and themes in raising consciousness and introduces two kinds of tools. The *lenses* of care, the generative life, and symbolic conduct provided ways for the participating managers to examine the organization and develop insights. The *platforms* or *bottom lines* of humanistic criteria, operational criteria, and productivity criteria provided three standards against which to plan and evaluate progress. Although much of worth happened at this stage, it also revealed the idea-action gap: The reflective activities with encouragement to act did not by and large yield significant changes in individual or group behavior.

Chapter 3, Integrating Work and Learning, describes ideas and actions that took the project beyond the impasse of the first stage. We strove to introduce patterns of inquiry into the day-to-day work at La Tadeo. Action projects provided a concrete structure that created expectations for action and provided guidelines toward achieving a good mix of reflection and action. The Compass of Inquiry offered a simple strategy for combining reflection and action in language more accessible than the original Teaching for Understanding framework drawn from classroom contexts. These steps generated considerably more change toward revised styles of work and toward a culture of learning than had resulted from the first phase.

Chapter 4, Smart Cultures of Communication, focuses on a set of problems that emerged during the first and second phases. It became apparent that much of the culture of La Tadeo, old and new, emerged through patterns of communication. Moreover, effective use of action projects, bottom lines, and tools such as the Compass of Inquiry depended on fluent and thoughtful communication. Accordingly, it was important to focus on communication as such, introducing into La Tadeo culture a range of communicational tools and practices. These included the idea of Generative Conversations, a Ladder of Feedback to make processes of feedback less aversive and more productive, strategies for managing conflict, and others.

Chapter 5, Leadership for Learning, foregrounds the role of leadership in culture making. Recognizing that leaders at various levels influence greatly the micro-cultures around them, the initiative introduced tools for leadership style. Leadership traps were identified and caution about them encouraged. Leadership strategies such as Leadership through Questions and the Bermuda Triangle of Leadership were defined and cultivated. These steps helped some leaders to adopt practices and attitudes that favored a culture of learning.

Chapter 6, The Architecture of Growth, looks backstage at the pulleys and scaffolds needed to sustain the intervention. Reading the story so far, one might imagine a team of experts introducing tools and facilitating various group interactions. Something like this was the case, but with crucial details of organization. The experts came both from outside and within La Tadeo. The team of facilitators expanded by drawing on interested participants. A pattern of regular meetings, an established office, written materials, workshops, mini-courses, and other elements sustained the initiative.

Chapter 7, Toward a Culture of Learning, offers a summation of the extent to which Understanding for

Organizations achieved cultural change within particular offices and groups at La Tadeo. Three stories illustrate what happened at its best. However, the initiative was far from trouble free. A fourth story recounts a culture clash that occurred when the board of La Tadeo hired a reengineering firm to streamline procedures, cut costs and boost efficiency in the administration of La Tadeo.

Chapter 8, Understanding for Organizations, reviews the project from the perspectives of the four themes introduced in this chapter, assesses progress, and considers what might be done differently were this sort of intervention to be undertaken again. The book concludes with a few central connections to the literature on organizational development.

Finally, at the end of each chapter, a reflection and action box invites readers to ponder the ideas discussed and consider how those ideas might apply to their own contexts.

Reflection

What experience have you had of a good idea not getting into action? What went wrong and why?

Do you find a culture of learning around you in your work setting? In what ways yes, in what ways no?

When you have a leadership role (leading a group, facilitating a meeting, etc.), what do you do to establish a culture of learning? What might you do that works against such a culture?

Do you have time to learn in significant ways during the flow of work? Could you find new ways to do so?

What structures and strategies do you find in your work setting that create and support learning opportunities?

Action

What would you have to do to *make* a good idea work? Pick a worthwhile small-scale idea and make it happen!

Choose one action you can do day in, day out, that would help to create a culture of learning for yourself and those around you. Try to get in the habit of doing at least that one thing.

Pick something you would like to learn during the flow of work that would help you do better with, or feel better about, your professional work. Find ways to make a little time and space during the workday to advance that learning.

2. Cultivating Consciousness

A Weekend of Reflection

When does a project start? At no one moment of course. It starts with a question here, a conversation there, a memo to follow up, a serious vision proposed, entertained, and accepted. A project starts with a series of events of increasing commitment and energy, not a single event.

Yet, if we were to yield to the temptation to point to a single event, there is a natural candidate. One December weekend early in the development of Understanding for Organizations, the Rector of La Tadeo, the Vice-Rector for Management and Finances, others from La Tadeo including the researchers, and the team from Harvard Project Zero traveled to a cottage outside Bogotá to spend two days envisioning how the project might develop.

They had a lot to think about. As mentioned in chapter 1, a group of managers at La Tadeo had assembled the Blue Book, which outlined problematic areas of their administration that posed problems. Accomplishing a good diagnosis of the problems had been a seriously undertaken and technically well-structured enterprise. The puzzle was making the consequent recommendations work in the midst of the many pressing everyday tasks faced by the administrators of La Tadeo—a clear case of the idea-action gap.

With discussion, the problem became clearer. The managers needed to act, but they were inexperienced at acting together to solve problems. Yes, they had united to identify a long list of organizational areas that needed attention, but few if any had experiences in collaborating with colleagues to understand the deep causes of problems, experiment with solutions, and develop new approaches. La Tadeo researchers and upper management agreed that this new project would develop and support such strategies. Yet such a move would not come easily at La Tadeo. The organizational culture emphasized giving top-down solutions rather than involving stakeholders directly. As many managers noted to the researchers, there was no tradition of reflection about what problems really meant within the culture of La Tadeo and what made them persist.

Translated into the idiom of Understanding for Organizations, these were challenges of understanding in action. Not just the managers who conducted the initial diagnoses, but also many other administrators now needed to be part of the thinking and action. While a carefully wrought diagnosis could inform their reflections, they also needed to find their own understandings of the challenges close to them within La Tadeo. They needed to ponder and accept suggestions, or question them. Often, they might need to figure out their own best ways of acting.

One point became especially apparent during that December weekend. If administrators at La Tadeo were to become more proactive, they needed to have a clear view of the structure and culture around them, just as farmers need to be aware of local weather patterns, surrounding soils and successful seed planting strategies. So the weekend group brainstormed images, ideas, and strategies toward an effective program of innovation within the administration at La Tadeo.

They hoped for highly motivated people, good patterns of communication, processes carried out quickly, staff members helping each other, and a deep sense of community, all founded on a mutual understanding of one another and a practical understanding of how to get things done. After several rounds of trying to fit various ideas together, three key concepts emerged that provided a structure for starting Understanding for Organizations. Because helping people to see the organizational world around them was central, the group called these key concepts *lenses,* and named the three *care, symbolic conduct,* and the *generative life.*

The *care* lens asked managers to consider how they cared for others, processes, resources, and the organization generally through their behavior, and how others and the organization cared for them. The *symbolic conduct* lens drew the symbolic side of behavior in organizations to manager's attention—how people's words and actions communicated not only their immediate practical significance but also "side messages" about trust or distrust, confidence or fear, commitment or uncertainty. The *generative life* lens asked managers to consider how other individuals and groups at La Tadeo supported the generativity of their lives. They explored how the organization fostered creativity, discovery, and personal development, as well as how they did likewise for others and themselves.

The lenses became not just ways of raising consciousness but bases for organizing the project itself. The top administration invited the managers who had been working on the Blue Book to form three groups, one for each lens. This was a bold decision, because it stepped away from the traditional bottom line of cost-efficiency. The participants' mission involved:

- Exploring the meaning of the lens itself—how might one understand *care, symbolic conduct* and the *generative life.*
- Observing and interpreting administrative activities at La Tadeo through the lens.
- Taking action based on the understandings so gained— understanding in action.

Thus, the three lenses of care, symbolic conduct, and the generative life came to provide not only guiding concepts but also working groups for the first year of the initiative and beyond. Later in the course of the project, a fourth lens emerged, *manager as maestro*, which asked leader figures to think of themselves as artists and teachers. Another concept important for consciousness-raising developed later in the first year, a response to the emphasis in many organizations on bottom-line productivity. Participants in Understanding for Organizations were encouraged to think not in terms of one bottom line but three: humanistic, operational, and productivity. The rest of this chapter explores the meaning and application of the four lenses and the three bottom lines. Recalling the four themes introduced in chapter 1, these elements were culture-makers—tools and ideals that helped to foster a different way of thinking and acting at La Tadeo.

Roberto's Office

How can conceptual lenses such as care, symbolic conduct, and the generative life provide insight that leads to helpful action? It helps to have a case in point. Here is an illustration constructed from several different episodes at La Tadeo.

As usual, Roberto's office was jittering with activity. People jogged from desk to desk, phones rang, and occasionally Roberto boomed out, "Where's that memo?" "Will somebody just answer that!" "Please bring in the last reports from the budget department." "Clara, get those figures straight for the meeting with the Vice-Rector this afternoon."

A professor came in at that moment, asking for permission to use a bigger classroom for a contest he was staging between the students of two different courses he taught. No one paid any attention to him. Eventually he got mad and started shouting. Roberto had to come out of his inner office and calm the professor down.

That was business as usual in Roberto's office. In general Roberto had very little time to reflect on how to run his office better. When problems arose, he used short-term solutions but rarely examined or changed any of the office procedures. Most of the time, similar problems continued to arise. In their department meetings, Roberto and his colleagues often spoke about the need to change. Roberto's boss Gloria, who supervised several offices, even photocopied articles about management trends she and others had explored within the Blue Book group and sent the articles to Roberto and others. Roberto and a few other managers attended a workshop or two. But nothing much changed. Roberto continued to ensure that his office got its work done by maintaining high energy and putting out fires as they arose.

Roberto and Gloria both needed new ways to look at their situation. The lenses introduced at the beginning of the Understanding for Organizations initiative provided such ways.

The Lens of Care

Many factors could have contributed to the difficulties Roberto had in his office. Perhaps the office was understaffed. Maybe the staff members had not received adequate training in the use of computers. Maybe their computers, telephones and filing systems were out of date. The office space itself could have been too small and cramped. Or perhaps the office did not have someone whose job it was to deal with requests like the professor or to answer the telephone routinely. Any or all of these factors could have promoted the frenetic pace of the office and the difficulties Roberto had in managing it.

The *care* lens brought managers together to understand how to improve their handling of such factors. Through the lens, managers examined how they made decisions about using, allocating and protecting resources—human, financial, physical and technological—within the organization and its community. For example, groups of managers looked at issues such as the organization's recycling policies, the process of budgetary decision making, how office personnel were trained and mentored, and how new computer equipment was allocated. Because the university had a well-known tradition of protecting the environment, the concept of care had a deep importance for the participants. Managing with care meant acting in ways within the organizational environment that promoted a healthy organizational ecology—including attention to its people, equipment, funds and surrounding community.

If Roberto were to examine his office using the care lens, he might begin to see ways to improve his office. He might develop a different protocol according to which people would answer phones or greet people who came with requests. If he found that documents and memos moved forward slowly because many in his office did not understand how to best use a word processor, he might call in a tutor to support people's learning or locate openings in computer courses at La Tadeo. Roberto's boss Gloria might wonder if sending him to workshops and passing articles to him was a worthwhile strategy. Though it certainly showed care for Roberto and his situation, perhaps there were other paths to support his and his office's growth better.

As many project participants noted, care was important for two reasons. On one hand, care reframed difficult decisions that managers made by adding a humanistic and ecological dimensions. If a manager faced a decision about saving money in a budget, the lens of care asked her to evaluate other organizational resources that might suffer as a result: Would such a decision display caring for people? Does such a decision value and protect the organization's facilities? Secondly, the lens of care guided participants to think and act proactively in their organizational environments. Managers soon began to think about long term projects and actions that could better support people in their office or better allocate physical resources. They began to conceive projects that would reach out into the surrounding community of workers, families, and students. No longer were managers simply reacting to situations; instead, they were charting new directions that would foster care in the future.

In order to get a better purchase on care, managers like Roberto reflected on their current practice and considered ways to improve it using the lens of care. Managers shared their responses and planned actions that they could sustain over time. An example of the style of these reflection questions appears in the box.

Care in Action

In what ways are you currently acting and making decisions that:

- Support people by making them feel empowered, valued and assisting them to be the best they can be in their work?

- Use technology (computers, video equipment, phones, etc.) in efficient and thoughtful ways to improve the quality of your, your office's and the organization's work?

- Use physical resources (paper, furniture, space, etc.) in ways that promote conservation and support good work?

- Promote caring for the surrounding community and environment of the university?

What can you do to improve your strategies in these areas?

The Lens of Symbolic Conduct

When Roberto, in the space of a few minutes, issued a string of questions and commands like "Where's that memo?" and "Will somebody just answer that!" what was he saying? The messages directly concerned memos, telephones, and such. However, one can also read Roberto's behavior for what might be called the *side-messages* in his behavior, what his speech and actions signaled about his style, his commitments, his values, his aims. The side-messages were saying something like this: "I'm rushed. We're all rushed. We have too much to do. You all have to help me keep our noses above water!"

Even though Roberto was just going about his ordinary activities, even though he did not mean to send sweeping messages with his actions, inevitably he did so. We all do. And we all read others' behavior between the lines, interpreting behavior for its broader motives, attitudes, and commitments.

Symbolic conduct can be defined as follows. When people act, they ordinarily have an immediate purpose— managing an office situation, greeting a guest, getting some rest, promoting an idea, accomplishing a sale. Their actions seen in this light are their *direct conduct*. However, their actions can also be interpreted as signaling broad attitudes, beliefs, habits, viewpoints, and so on—from now on "attitudes" for short. Seen in this light, people's actions constitute *symbolic conduct*. Also included in symbolic conduct are the side-signals sent by physical traces of behavior—a door left open or closed, the closing phrase of a letter, a style of clothing. Bolman and Deal, in their *Reframing Organizations,* define a similar concept as one of four frames through which to analyze organizational behavior. In keeping with Bolman and Deal, groups and organizations also display symbolic conduct. For instance, an organization's introduction of comprehensive health benefits not only accomplishes that immediate aim but also makes a statement of caring and concern, especially if reinforced by similar actions in other areas.

Why does symbolic conduct matter? The answer connects back to one of the principle themes of this book, culture-makers. Cultural commitments get expressed through patterns of symbolic conduct. Consider Roberto's conduct again. It expresses what one might call a culture of immediacies. Roberto, and those he leads, deal with the affairs of the office as they arise, with little attention to long-term improvement. The culture of immediacies in Roberto's office is anything but a culture of learning!

But symbolic conduct is more than an expression of culture. It is also a creator of culture. Recall, in fact, that one of the culture-makers mentioned in chapter 1 was *actions*. A new worker in Roberto's office would quickly pick up the dominant culture by reading people's symbolic conduct. The old-timers in Roberto's office find the dominant culture reinforced on all sides by others' actions, and participate in reinforcing it themselves. Symbolic conduct tends to sustain the dominant culture, for better or worse.

However, this does not mean that a culture is fixed in place forever. Cultures do change. The right kinds of actions can introduce and nourish a new culture. Recalling chapter 1 again, leaders are also culture makers. Indeed, much of their power to make culture comes from the actions they take and the messages those actions broadcast. Roberto, with the right kind of insight and coaching, could become such a leader, helping himself and his office to escape from a culture of immediacies toward a culture of learning.

It was in this spirit that the Symbolic Conduct Group formed and began to explore the implications of symbolic conduct for La Tadeo. But more specifically, how might one go about looking at an organizational situation from the perspective of symbolic conduct?

Reading Symbolic Conduct

What do the side messages seem to be in this conduct? That is, what does the conduct say about attitude, commitments, expectations, etc.?

Who do the side messages say it about?—The individual, a group, an office culture, the whole organization (perhaps more than one)?

How reliable are the messages? Do they speak a truth about the actor, or might they mislead—for instance as in token approval or token participation?

And very important: *Are there alternative readings?* Very often conduct is ambiguous, interpretable in more than one way. We project our expectations on another's behavior and confirm our prejudices. What is the evidence for the validity of one reading versus another?

The Symbolic Conduct Group often found it useful to focus on what might be called *hotspots* in the flow of work. These were aspects of office activity that proved revealing of the underlying culture and often problematic. Hotspots might differ from setting to setting. In Roberto's office, a hotspot might concern Roberto's command style, in another office, a hotspot might concern collaboration, and in another, how medium-term decisions got made. With a hotspot in front of the lens, questions like those in the box are useful in reading the symbolic conduct in play.

The Lens of the Generative Life

Roberto's boss Gloria wanted to give Roberto a chance to express his best personality traits and to draw on his academic background and creativity. She understood that her managerial style in the past had conditioned Roberto to adopt a routine work style that might have hindered organizing the office activities in a more dynamic and creative way. Gloria had been reflecting on the concept of the generative life, and she felt ready to explore how it might help others around her to grow and find fulfillment in the workplace.

Generative life is a concept that relates to personal and professional well-being. It was defined by La Tadeo participants in the lens group on the generative life as:

> ...a life in which the attitudes towards life itself and towards others are positive, constructive and optimistic. A generative life implies that the individual has a vision of life where permanent growth, creativity, happiness, well-being and productivity are principal objectives. The different areas of a person's life become balanced through the continuing effort to reflect, know oneself, assume responsibilities, allow oneself to be creative, learn from mistakes, accumulate experience, and be mindful. You as an individual take charge of your life and shape it to what you expect from it instead of letting circumstances decide your fate.

Managers touched by this concept fostered around them a change in attitude and cultivated enthusiasm and commitment. Roberto's superior called him in, and, much to his astonishment, he heard her saying that he should be dreaming about new ways to engage in his work. She proposed that he attend the next *Encuentro,* a kind of course offered from time to time as part of Understanding for Organizations (see chapter 6). Roberto was pleased with the opportunity, although a bit puzzled by the new attitude Gloria had displayed.

A couple of months later, Gloria visited Roberto's office. The frenetic pace had been replaced by relative calm, and people seemed happy doing their work. "Good to see you. Would you like a coffee," said the secretary, whom Gloria remembered as bad-tempered. "Roberto is talking to a professor who wants to set up a special event for his students. I'll tell him that you're here."

Roberto asked Gloria in and, after greetings, Roberto quickly arrived at a solution with the professor. Saying goodbye, he turned to Gloria.

"So what's new around here?" asked Gloria.

"Well," Roberto responded, "I've made a few changes. All the staff members meet once a week. We've come to know each other better professionally and also personally. Now everybody knows what others in the office are doing. We've come up with some ways to make things easier for one another individually, and now we're developing some group projects.

"What about getting it all done? Have people had to put in extra hours to get together and how do they feel about that?" asked Gloria.

"Actually we have more time now," responded Roberto. "I've made some changes in the procedures. We've coordinated with other offices and figured out ways to speed up both ends of the work."

As with the lenses of care and symbolic conduct, managers began to better understand how to foster a generative life though considering questions. In the box on the preceding page are some typical questions the

The Generative Life Examined

Do you allow yourself and your staff to look at work as a source of opportunities to grow?

Are you happy and enthusiastic about your life?

How true to your ideals is the life you are leading? Can it be improved? How so?

What do you see around you in your office? Are people motivated? Are they growing and learning at work?

Are you mindfully assuming your responsibilities or are the external circumstances deciding for you?

managers used to reflect and devise changes in their work practices.

The Work of the Lens Groups

With the lenses themselves described, it's worth recounting how groups of managers focusing on each of the three lenses advanced Understanding for Organizations. Beginning in the spring of the first year of the project, the researchers invited 25 office managers to explore and apply the lenses of care, symbolic conduct, and the generative life. These managers were the same ones who met regularly in the months before to identify the organizational challenges in the Blue Book. Using the pedagogical framework Teaching for Understanding as a point of departure (see chapter 1), the researchers introduced the lenses to the managers as a way to address many of their main concerns. For example, the managers had concluded that the organization needed to improve physical and technological resources, which lent itself to the lens of care; communications, which lent itself to the lens of symbolic conduct; and institutional commitment, which lent itself to the lens of generative life. In the initial meeting with the managers, the project researchers previewed the lenses, and managers voluntarily signed up to a lens that most interested them.

Each lens group had an on-site facilitator who organized the meetings and conversations and documented the group's progress. The Symbolic Conduct Group and the Generative Life Group were each led by a part-time project researcher. In contrast, a highly placed university manager, who had proposed the care lens, led the Care Group. Each lens group facilitator teamed up with an off-site Harvard researcher who, through emails, telephone calls, faxes and video tapes of meetings, kept abreast of each group's development and offered counsel.

In what soon became the ritual meeting time for the project, every Friday morning each lens group convened separately to explore, define, refine and apply their lens. About every six weeks, the groups met together to share advances and hear new ideas from one another. Although the groups had much in common, each charted its own distinctive course. For example, the Care Group began by asking themselves, "What does care mean at La Tadeo?" Managers in the group already knew each other and brought in stories from their practice from which they developed criteria for care. With criteria in hand, the lens group evolved a project-centered approach. The participating managers each applied the criteria by developing office projects that aimed to display care in the organization. The projects included designing an organizational recycling policy, creating a new technology service department, helping environmental student groups, redesigning the university's laboratories, and developing better audio/visual services. Every week, different offices presented their projects, shared advances, raised puzzles and gathered feedback from the group.

The Symbolic Conduct Group began with ideas of what symbolic conduct meant based on writings by one of the Project Zero researchers. The group raised their awareness of symbolic conduct by examining their practice. The participants engaged in activities to sharpen their abilities to recognize and alter their symbolic conduct. The facilitator brought in videos, created worksheets and guided case discussions in which participants examined symbolic acts. Managers brought in and examined stories and events from La Tadeo asking questions like, "What are the side messages?" and "How do we know we're reading them accurately?" After a few months, managers developed personal projects that aimed to improve their management of symbolic conduct. For example, one participant created a project on improving his actions to communicate teamwork and commitment better. Another manager focused on creating organizational actions such as seminars, fairs and databases to better display an emphasis on research throughout the university.

The Generative Life Group also commenced with a basic definition. Similar to the symbolic conduct group, many of the participants did not know each other very well. To create a supportive and honest environment, the group began by sharing their personal hobbies and stories about themselves and their families. Group members soon began to write and share reflections about their personal dreams and professional aspirations. Through questions such as, "Do I feel as though I have opportunities to grow? Do I have a chance to live up to my ideals? Are others around me motivated and learning?" they examined their values, thinking habits and attitudes. Such interactions led the group to refine their ideas about what a generative life and a generative organization meant at La Tadeo. The group then looked at the microclimates in their offices and in the organization. They created a rubric that evaluated how these microclimates supported or thwarted a generative life. Finally, based on evaluations, the participants developed projects to improve the generativity in their office microclimates and in the organization. Such projects included making user-friendly manuals to help guide clients, teaming up with other offices to get to know them better and to work on issues and processes they shared, and personal projects such as controlling anger.

The Impact of the Lens Groups

For about a year and a half, the lens groups provided the main working structures for Understanding for Organizations, eventually giving way to other structures (see chapter 6). The researchers investigated the impact systematically using interviews, office observations, focus groups and rating scales, as well as documenting individual and group projects that the participants undertook. The following italics represent questions the researchers directly observed and asked.

A survey towards the end of this phase of the project revealed that the managers felt the lenses greatly *elevated their inclinations to change (100% of managers reporting this)* and made them much more *aware of others' contribution to the organization (95.5%)*. Managers reported that the strategy *heightened awareness of the importance for valuing and supporting others (95.5%)*. Along with fostering such awareness, participants noted that the lens groups directly *created more space and time for personal and professional reflection (86.4%)*. And perhaps most significantly, the researchers and participants alike concluded that the lens groups enabled participants to form small and trusting communities with particular identities. This seemed to lead to improved internal communication and relationships among the managers. Managers commented in interviews and focus group meetings how valuable the lenses were because the lenses enabled them to learn about different facets of their colleagues. They said that such personal knowledge and familiarity helped them collaborate and solve problems better.

However, many difficulties arose. The lenses led many managers to be clearer about policies that were not working. Often times when higher-ups and colleagues who were supposedly supporting the project made bad decisions or displayed poor attitudes, project members felt betrayed and discouraged, and they voiced their anger with the organization in group meetings. Some managers expressed a cynical view of what the leadership of the organization was saying: "It is important for you all to understand these issues of care, symbolic conduct, and generative life. But we will continue to act as we please." The researchers felt that this accounted for much acrimony and potential rifts early in the project. The surveys after a year and a half of exploring lenses revealed this sense. Just over half of the managers reported that they seriously questioned the organization's will for real change.

Overall, the lens groups served as the first line of robust exploration for the project managers. As the project developed, the researchers moved beyond lens groups and began to involve managers in inquiry through Encuentros and understanding-in-action groups (see chapter 6). One reason for this change of strategy was that the project sought to explore different structures that best facilitated managers learning. Another reason was that, as managers began to share their insights of the lens within the larger group, participants became eager to understand all the lenses equally.

Manager as Maestro

Maestro is an interesting Spanish word. It means both master (as in an orchestra conductor, who is a "maestro" in Italian and English) and teacher. With this in mind, "manager as maestro" might almost seem to be an oxymoron. Another oxymoron in the same spirit is "leader as teacher." We do not ordinarily think of managers or leaders in the role of teachers. They have other things to do: managing and leading.

Yet as Understanding for Organizations advanced, plenty of reasons emerged to urge the participating managers to think of themselves as teachers. Recall again the theme of leader as culture maker. People in managerial positions are culture makers whether they think of themselves as such or not. Whether they do any direct mentoring or not, their actions powerfully shape the culture around them through the immediate effects of those actions and through symbolic conduct. To invite managers to think of themselves as maestros is to encourage them to be aware of how their actions teach. It is to encourage them to shape their actions to teach lessons that will advance the well-being and effectiveness of the people under them.

In fullest form, the manager as maestro is an ideal. He or she is the gardener, the cultivator, the inciter, a source of inspiration and wisdom, and an impetus to learn and to develop toward effective autonomy. The maestro is sometimes tender, sometimes pungent as the occasion demands. The maestro leads the Socratic dialogue that brings to light or converts into action the potentials that people carry within themselves.

Another more specific reason recommended the lens of the maestro. The three lenses of care, symbolic conduct, and the generative life often offered complementary visions of the same phenomena. How could they be combined? Perhaps by way of the thought and actions of the maestro. Consider the lens of care for example. The ideal maestro offers care and cultivates the giving of care by others. Care within La Tadeo or any other organization has human, social, and political aspects, material and spiritual concerns, at the level of the individual, the group, and the community. Care involves not just being careful about people and their feelings, but careful about processes and products. To be broadly careful is not to submit easily to what is urgent or politically sound when something else is better logistically or technically.

The ideal maestro teaches through symbolic conduct, functioning as a living symbol of autonomy, growth, responsibility, self-esteem and creativity. At La Tadeo, it was important for managers to become aware of the symbolic content of their actions. When this happened, managers not only began to read the scene more acutely but also began to understand what their own actions expressed to others and reconsider what messages they really wanted to send. Finally, as to the generative life, the ideal maestro helps to create a generative life for those who work with him or her. The maestro promotes the creation of personal, group or organizational projects that advance both individuals and the organization. The maestro fosters a culture open to creativity and initiatives that foreground a sound emotional life and well-founded humane belief system and values.

The history of manager as maestro differs from that of the care, symbolic conduct, and generative life lenses. Manager as maestro emerged part way through the first year, in response to a suggestion from the Rector. A group never formed around manager as maestro, because participants had already found their group affiliations. However, the concept of manager as maestro received considerable attention as the project advanced. In small groups and larger meetings, participants brought forward their ideas about manager as maestro, as well as examples and counterexamples of maestro-like behavior. Manager as maestro became a member in good standing of the project's conceptual repertoire and a source of guidance for the participants. The ideas and tools in chapter 5, Leadership for Learning, offer a range of ways that people in positions of leadership can teach through their actions and interactions.

Bottom Lines, Plural

Rosaline, a manager in one of the lens groups, began to ask herself how she evaluated the success of her office. Like many of her colleagues, she often looked for evidence of how quickly projects got finished and how smoothly her office could deal with challenges that arose. But she also paid keen attention to how people felt about their work. Whether people felt valued, empowered and motivated played an important part in her assessment of office success.

So what were the bottom lines in the organization? This familiar question asks us to consider, as did Rosaline, how things balance out to a net result. Taken literally, the bottom line has to do with balance sheets—in the black, in the red, and by how much? Taken metaphorically, the bottom line has to do with any hard-nosed assessment of the final condensed outcome or essence of something.

The hegemony of the bottom line is a familiar feature of organizational settings. And not without some justification! The bottom line plays a fundamental role in any management process. Ultimately, benefits need to match or exceed costs, whether with reference to money or less tangible indices of productivity. That said, the bottom line of productivity considered in isolation tends to neglect fundamental aspects of human relations, organizational procedures and structures, and more—factors that feed the productivity bottom line. Rosaline's reflection resonates with this conclusion.

It became clear to the investigative team that the productivity bottom line was important at La Tadeo, as in any organization. Some functions of the administration were not as productive as they could be relative to invested cost and human effort. How, then, could Understanding for Organizations focus on productivity? By when might it yield clear gains in productivity? Questions like these were asked by the advocates of the project from the beginning, and even more aggressively by the skeptics.

Such questions demanded a response. The response was to acknowledge and plan for impact on the classic bottom line of productivity—but not only that. To broaden the perspective beyond productivity, the project team introduced two other bottom lines, making a trio of *humanistic, operational,* and *productivity* bottom lines. The three constituted a potent set of ideals for organizational development. As stated in chapter 1, ideals, when attended to seriously in a context, become culture-makers.

- The *humanistic bottom line* established as a general standard the importance of managers organizing their work around an understanding of the underlying system of values, beliefs, principles, attitudes and feelings that shapes work and relationships in an organization.

- The *operational bottom line* established as a general standard the importance of effective and efficient processes, methods, and settings within an organization. Operational features include how and how well decisions are made, information is shared, rules and policies are formulated and implemented, procedures are carried out, and so on.
- The *productivity bottom line* acknowledged as a general standard the importance of output: the products and achievements, monetary and otherwise, of the organization or unit within the organization. It asked managers to conceive their plans for innovation in ways that reflected an understanding of how such outcomes occurred and how they might better occur. It also encouraged examining how such products are shared, viewed, and judged within the organization and the surrounding community.

Recall that people asked not only whether the Understanding for Organization project attended to the bottom line, but when results could be expected. A useful answer could be given in terms of the three bottom lines. Organizational theorist Peter Senge noted during a conference the typical path of organizational development, describing it in terms analogous to the three bottom lines. Senge averred that many innovations first affect the humanistic bottom line. People become more sensitive and able in managing themselves and their relationships with others. Then, building on this foundation over a period of months, people turn to operational improvements. A while later, the operational improvements translate into gains in productivity. While the temptation always is to look for productivity gains first, or at least simultaneously with humanistic and operational gains, this does not reflect the realities of human psychology or organizational change. The productivity gains are there to be had, but the causal chain of events takes a while to get to them.

The three bottom lines cannot always be measured by exact numbers—not even the productivity bottom line, unless the kind of productivity in question concerns money, and many other kinds of productivity were relevant within La Tadeo—for instance, the throughput of an office. Nonetheless, all three were thought of as measurable in a rough way, through the use of various performance indicators. Particular initiatives—for instance, the action projects to be discussed in the next chapter—might place more or less emphasis on the different bottom lines, and any initiative could be appraised with reference to all three. And any balanced set of initiatives taken collectively should address all three.

Assessment Using the Bottom Lines

While formally evaluating initiatives was one application of the three bottom lines, the researchers discovered that the bottom lines also provided a powerful interpretive tool. Programs and events within La Tadeo could be examined and assessed informally, using the bottom lines as lenses. This often proved quite revealing.

The Case of the Purchasing Innovation

For example, at one point the Systems department and the Rector introduced a new technological system for making the purchasing process more flexible and efficient. This was an important and ultimately advantageous innovation, but pitfalls occurred along the way. The team introducing the system had to devise a process for the whole community to learn how to use it. This seemed quite easy at first. The team organized a two-week training program including the entire management area, expecting to have the system working throughout La Tadeo after two weeks. However, what actually happened diverged from their expectations in ways readily charted by the bottom lines.

From the perspective of the humanistic bottom line, the introduction did not take into account the fact that most of the people did not have any training with computers. Many were a little fearful of using them. The training also did not consider the distinctive roles of those invited and formed groups with people in different hierarchical positions within the organization. Some of the managers in higher positions were embarrassed when those in lower positions discovered that they were not knowledgeable about the innovation.

From the perspective of the operational bottom line, the training occurred off site. This was convenient for the training itself. However, many participants found themselves using computers different from those in their offices, and some participants did not even have computers in their offices. Also, at some points, the training assumed that the participating managers knew the by-hand version of certain routine processes in detail. However, it was the secretaries who usually, and appropriately, carried out these processes. The managers were clueless about what the training meant or how to use it.

As to the productivity bottom line, the net result was negative. The new system was not implemented in the time anticipated. Much of the training time and cost was lost. The purchasing process, in the short term, became slower and also more error prone, because users entered mistaken information into the system.

However, these difficulties did pose a learning opportunity that had real value. While reflecting on and receiving feedback about the process, the manager of the training operation formulated an alternative solution that could have served better and might inform future efforts. On the humanistic side, the initial training could have focused on people who knew about and were interested in computers, who had computers in their offices, and who felt motivated by the innovation and eager to collaborate. Operationally, by beginning with a small group, the conductors of the training could have identified possible difficulties and corrected them before a larger scale effort. Those who had received early training and testing might train in-office secretaries or others that normally played a role in the purchasing processes. From a productivity standpoint, this would have meant paying for fewer hours of training per group, losing no time training people who did not need to be trained, and ensuring that the new process became practical much earlier.

The Culture and the Bottom Lines

Useful for examining particular episodes, the bottom lines also afforded perspectives from which to appraise general cultural patterns within La Tadeo. They provided another way of viewing many of the challenges that had earlier been identified in the Blue Book and some of the factors underlying them.

Viewing La Tadeo from the humanistic perspective, the researchers observed that participants, quite understandably, were much more sensitive to others' symbolic conduct than their own. No organization can give everybody everything they need. However, when something was given to one person, others often read this as symbolic conduct disparaging to them. Patterns of jealousy and low self-esteem emerged. In the hierarchical organization of La Tadeo, a tradition of automatic obedience tended to inhibit the empowerment of individuals. When such individuals acted, they more often did so in response to repeated requests than to revised understandings. When advances occurred, they appeared in larger or smaller pockets rather than throughout the community.

Considering the operational bottom line, effective operations require reflective understanding. In many settings within La Tadeo, a culture of reflection competed poorly with the time pressures of the everyday workflow. One manager even commented that he felt "addicted to action." Thinking things over felt like idleness. Such mindsets led managers to lose sensitivity to moments that especially required reflection, often finding themselves swept away by complex situations or swept along by habitual routines. The more immediate the demands, the more many managers tended to revert to practices that inhibited inquiry and understanding in the workplace, even though a stand-back response might have helped.

Many offices at La Tadeo had deeply entrenched processes. These practices involved patterns of work flow not focused on client or market, making the introduction of new ideas difficult. Some managers noted, "Things have always been done that way, with good results!" Another force inhibiting improvement of operations might be called a culture of silence. Information was generated but not used. Managers proposed projects with no response either of support or critique. Such lack of reaction inevitably reduced motivation and proactivity and made it difficult to inspire people to conceive and pursue dreams. A further and final obstacle to improved operations was the committee system, which tended to dilute the responsibility of leaders to support some innovations firmly.

As to the productivity bottom line, results that are not documented, analyzed and found valuable tend to get lost in organizations. At La Tadeo, workers commonly accomplished worthwhile results that hardly anyone else knew about. Documenting outcomes would not just have yielded personal benefits. An organization that loses the history of what has been done tends to repeat its mistakes and fail to repeat its successes. A small detail lost in the shuffle might end up costing huge amounts of money next year. It is commonplace, but certainly unfortunate, that organizations do not register and appraise products and results with care and precision outside of competitive situations. When the market shrinks or a competitor emerges, then people take a hard look. Short of that, excellent results mix with haphazard results, with no one taking much note of the difference.

These remarks on salient cultural shortfalls of La Tadeo demonstrate the kinds of insights the three bottom lines helped to generate. They certainly should not be taken as singling out La Tadeo for special criticism. Difficulties such as those mentioned are quite common in large organizations. Nor should they be taken as presenting a uniformly grim profile. Traps that one office or individual might fall into, the office or individual next door might evade, demonstrating thoughtful work and fine results. Nor should they be taken as saying that the kinds of shortfalls mentioned are inevitable. Indeed, a central purpose of Understanding for Organizations was to do better.

From Awareness to Action

The original lenses of care, symbolic conduct, and the generative life, the further lens of manager as maestro, and the three bottom lines—humanistic, operational, and productive—all served as tools for elevating the consciousness of participants in Understanding for Organizations. Many participants learned to see the organizational world around them more keenly and deeply by using several of these conceptual resources. Their amplified awareness put them in a good position not only to discern problems and opportunities but also to generate initiatives in response.

All this was important and encouraging. Nonetheless, the researchers observed that, for many participants, moving to concrete action posed yet another barrier. Despite thoughtful discussions and articulate plans, the idea-action gap made its presence known. Indeed, some participants seemed ready to ruminate forever, although others proved more proactive. With the idea-action gap in mind, beginning in the summer of the first year of the project, the researchers introduced further tools that focused attention on concrete action. These are the topics of the next chapter.

Reflection

Choose one of the three lenses—care, symbolic conduct, or the generative life—and examine the activities around you through that lens. What do you see? What do you like and not like about what you see?

Look at your own behavior from the perspectives of care, symbolic conduct, and the generative life. What are you most happy with and what would you most like to change?

Who around you functions as a "maestro?" What can you learn from that person?

Consider your setting from the perspective of the bottom lines. What is the balance of attention among humanistic, operational, and productivity bottom lines, and is the balance appropriate?

Action

Form a small group to consider your organizational setting, using one or all of the lenses.

Choose a pattern of behavior that you would like to change using the lenses. Select something tractable, and invest a little effort in changing it.

Choose a context where you have some influence—perhaps a meeting you lead or a small group in which you participate—and through your actions introduce shifts in the balance between humanistic, operational, and productivity concerns.

3. Integrating Work and Learning

The Three Fridays

Midway through the project, for three consecutive Friday mornings, La Tadeo managers gathered together in a large university classroom. At the invitation of the university Rector and Vice-Rector for Management and Finances, the managers shared and gave feedback to each office's yearly plan. However, these plans differed from the usual budgetary planning that many managers had done in the past. These plans asked managers explicitly to integrate learning into office practices. Groups took turns displaying posters on the classroom walls that articulated the dreams the managers had for their offices. Each poster listed the particular puzzles to be solved and how the managers wanted to grow. The managers also included the actions the office would take and how the office would evaluate success. In other words, managers of each office presented a plan of what they wanted to understand in action in the course of the coming year.

During the first half hour of these Friday meetings, managers silently circulated around the classroom, read the posters and wrote reactions and questions on blank feedback sheets posted next to each poster. Many managers took personal notes about the patterns they saw across offices. Afterwards, the managers assembled in small groups to share what they noticed and wondered about. To conclude, managers came together as a large group to point out interesting and valuable ideas they observed in the process. They voiced general concerns and offered suggestions about how all offices might better put their understanding into action.

The Rector and the Vice-Rector for Management and Finances, who attended these sessions, observed how this experience not only brought the group together as a community but also enabled the managers to appreciate the value learning had in the organization. "One advantage of these meetings is that we all get to know what the different offices are doing. We see how we can interact by giving feedback and planning our actions in a more coordinated way," summarized the Vice-Rector. "But also, it has given the managers and myself the idea that work is an opportunity for learning and growth. Every decision we make and every action we take are moments from which we can learn better. We now see that what we as an organization need to do is support people to improve their learning as they work. And there are many challenges to achieve this."

As the Vice-Rector pointed out, integrating learning into work—the third of the four themes introduced in chapter 1—is a perennial challenge in organizational settings. One reason for this is that people too often view learning as removed from the flow of work. Managers in the project at La Tadeo noted that learning was not something they considered as part of their everyday work experience. Rather they saw learning as something that happened in workshops, seminars, or classes outside of the work. Certainly experiences removed from the harried pace of work are important. At their best, such experiences offer access to a wealth of new ideas, strategies, and information. However, as chapter 1 pointed out, learning outside of the workflow does little to close the idea-action gap. Ideas introduced in classrooms or seminars too often prove difficult to import into the flow of work and too fragile to sustain over time.

From the standpoint of learning theory, this can be considered a problem of transfer of learning. A considerable body of research shows that concepts and practices learned in one context often do not transfer readily to others where in principle they apply. Effective transfer commonly depends on organizing the learning experience in ways that foster it, rather than assuming that transfer will occur automatically. The kind of transfer sought here depends largely on a culture of work where learning becomes fused with daily actions, not separate from them.

Integrating learning into the flow of work is not a new or radical concept. Over the years, many researchers have written about the need for learning in action, and obstacles inherent it. Kurt Lewin, the pioneering social researcher of the 1940s, articulated many such ideas in his platform of action research. More recently, George Washington University's Nancy Dixon has reawakened the need for integrating learning into organizational life. Donald Schön did the same through his notion of the reflective practitioner. These authors all agree that integrating learning into work lies at the heart of smart action and professional growth.

This chapter will unveil strategies that project investigators developed to integrate learning into work at La Tadeo. To begin with, the chapter will outline the "work as inquiry" philosophy that the project sought to cultivate. The chapter will introduce a language that managers used to initiate and support learning at work. It will then explain in detail the methods of action projects—personal and group journeys of inquiry—that managers designed to integrate learning into their workflow. As a conclusion the chapter will provide examples and evidence of impact gathered by the researchers.

Work as Inquiry

Imagine that you attended the Three Fridays. There, forty or so managers mingled, read, and made observations. Each manager examined the goals, questions and annual learning plan of the others. They offered criticisms and gave suggestions to support their colleagues' learning. Clearly, this was about work: The meeting concerned what each participant did and would do in the organization. But the view of work was not so usual. It foregrounded reflection, action, and feedback. It focused on learning through an inquiry approach to work.

During a summer workshop early in the project, the researchers introduced managers to an organizing philosophy of integrating learning into their work: *work as inquiry*. As mentioned earlier, many managers found it difficult to envision learning as part of work. A few managers even voiced worries that learning on the job could be seen as time-consuming and unprofessional, considering the never-ending flow of work that needed attention. To stretch these limited perspectives of learning in work, the session invited managers to consider their work—their daily actions, interactions, roles and responsibilities—as something more than simple rote and repetitive behaviors. Instead, managers were called upon to envision their work as a journey of inquiry, a journey with much to be explored, learned, and understood in action. As a core value, *work as inquiry* urged managers to design and organize their work in ways that yielded gains in knowledge and understanding.

Many managers reported that work as inquiry openly challenged them to improve their way of thinking and acting in their professional contexts. Almost all managers agreed that such a shared core value was important to the project. That is why, on those three Fridays, many managers stayed late, exchanging ideas and feedback to fuel the inquiry process. However, having a core value is not enough. Infusing learning into work required the project to create a language that supported inquiry.

A Language for Learning at Work

If you were strolling around the room during the Three Fridays, you would find that the managers' posters stated their plans for learning in terms of four categories. One poster read as follows:

Dreams

My dream is to create the best audio/visual service possible for teachers and students.

Mysteries

How do I get feedback from the students and teachers about the service I'm providing?

How can I know about the materials that teachers are using or need to use for their courses?

How can I make scheduling easier for teachers and students?

How can I prepare the people who work with me for the best use of the resources we have?

Actions

Create a suggestion box for students and teachers who use the resources.

Conduct interviews with teachers to find out about their needs.

Devise a schedule in coordination with the different departments who use the service.

Develop in-depth training for our workers and have them conduct mini-action projects.

Evidence

Make observations of students' behaviors and attitudes toward the Audiovisual Department.

The comments made by customers will provide data to make adjustments or new plans.

The mini-action projects made by workers.

Dreams, mysteries, actions, evidence... what was this about? The researchers had introduced and refined a language to help the managers plan and enact learning at work. This framework of four key ideas guided them as a Compass of Inquiry, with its four primary directions, helping them to hone in on their desired destinations. Lessons from prior research had shown that the original Teaching for Understanding (TfU) language was cumbersome. As mentioned in chapter 1, the TfU language was originally crafted for the classroom. It made sense to teachers, assisting them in creating curricula and learning experiences for their students. However, the researchers at La Tadeo soon found that its key vocabulary did not match organizational context. Therefore, the researchers designed, piloted, and refined a different key vocabulary based on the same concepts: formulating *dreams* and *mysteries,* planning and undertaking *actions* that pursued those dreams and mysteries, and gathering *evidence* of progress. At first, the researchers were skeptical that this deliberately somewhat poetic quartet of terms would connect well with serious-minded managers. But the managers reported in surveys and interviews that such a language easily reflected their work, better supported and inspired them in moving to action, and encouraged them to strengthen the personal connections to their work.

Though the language of the Compass of Inquiry appears here in a linear order—*dreams, mysteries, actions, evidence*—it is important to note that the managers started at different entry points when formulating their inquiry. Most commenced with dreams, but some with mysteries. A few began by considering actions. Where a manager started was not important, so long as the four areas came together in a fully developed plan to integrate learning into work.

Dreams

What did the managers really want to do? What were their dreams, their hopes and their goals for themselves and La Tadeo? Answers to such questions defined the dreams—or, less poetically, goals, aspirations and objectives—worth pursuing. Creating these dreams enabled the managers to connect their daily experiences to what they most wanted to achieve. Their dreams generated personal and organizational meaning for their inquiry. Managers' dreams took many different shapes and sizes. Some managers articulated personal life-long dreams; others formulated professional dreams for the upcoming month. Over time, many dreams shifted and evolved. Whether they were personal, professional, long or short term, individual or collective, the dreams inspired and focused learning at work.

By way of example, some of the dreams on the posters hung up during the three Friday Sessions were "improving the physical plant services," "to create commitment and respect throughout the university," "to better organize my and my office's time," and "to offer better courses and training to the university employees."

Mysteries

What puzzled the managers as they thought about working toward their dreams? What were their questions? What did they want to understand better about themselves or the organization? Answers to such questions were their mysteries, puzzles, and enigmas, matters that called for understanding in action. The mysteries defined areas for the managers to investigate, understand, and construct new insights for themselves and others in the organization. Articulating the mysteries aroused the sustained curiosity needed for meaningful inquiry.

Mysteries that appeared on the Friday posters included questions such as "What are the physical plant needs?" "What are the current strategies to solve them?" "How can commitment and respect be built?" "How can people get to know each other better?" "What prevents me from using my time well?" and "What courses do the university employees want to take?"

Actions

What cycles of actions would help advance their dreams? What actions would resolve their mysteries? Such questions asked the managers to formulate and pursue plans of action. Simply stating dreams and mysteries was not enough. Managers needed to act. Behaving in the same old way would not change anything nor build new understandings. Managers had to engage in cycles of novel and revealing actions.

Some actions that managers shared during the three Fridays were "take photos of the university and talk with managers to assess physical plant needs," "experiment with an assessment tool to profile what commitment and respect look like in an office," "observe my office environment and take notes of the interruptions in my work," and "create and administer a questionnaire that asks employees about their interest in courses."

Dreams	Mysteries
What do we really want to achieve? What visions, goals, aspirations, or objectives do we strive to realize?	What are our questions, worries, enigmas, or aspects of a situation that we want to understand to achieve the dreams?

Compass of Inquiry

Evidence	Actions
What do we look at to evaluate progress? What feedback, data, or observations gauge our advancement toward attaining our dreams and resolving our mysteries?	What might we do to achieve the dreams and understand the mysteries? What cycles of actions, plans, processes or activities should we engage in?

How would managers know if their actions were working towards their dreams and informing their mysteries? This final category called upon managers to collect evidence—data, observations, and feedback from different sources that gauged progress towards their dreams and mysteries. Carrying out actions with evidence would allow the managers to track their growth, improve their performances, and share their progress with others.

Examples of evidence that managers gathered through their action projects and displayed during the three Fridays included "physical plant portfolios with pictures taken over time to document changes," "data from employees to see if the climate of respect and commitment in their office changes," "changes in behavior that show how I trust others and delegate responsibility to better use my time," and "analyzing the data and feedback from employees about courses."

Camilo's Learning at Work

What does it look like to use this language of inquiry in practice? How did managers articulate and act upon their dreams, mysteries, actions and evidence? The case of Camilo illustrates these ideas in action. Camilo, like many university managers, worked closely with a project researcher, who documented his progress over time.

Camilo had been in the university for over 15 years. He felt his quality of work in the organization was good. He was known for his calm style. His office reflected his demeanor: Routines were well-established and few problems typically arose. Every Monday he assembled his office together to outline the week's work and things generally flowed well.

One day, in a meeting with his boss and other managers, Camilo received a set of questions to be answered about their offices, questions like, "How do your customers feel about the service you offer?" "What changes have you made to the service in the last two years?" "What do you feel proud of in your work?" "What are your major concerns?" These questions stirred him deeply. He had never wondered what his clients thought. He had never considered making changes. He had never asked himself what he felt proud of. He had only focused on doing what had to be done.

Camilo's boss encouraged him to integrate learning into his workflow as a way to change the culture in the department. With a small number of his colleagues, he met with a project researcher who explained the Compass language of dreams, mysteries, actions and evidence. He noticed some excitement among his colleagues: They hadn't thought seriously about those things either. Full of energy, Camilo returned to his office. On that next Monday, he asked each of the members of his staff to write down on a piece of paper the things they would like to improve in their work. Camilo invited his office workers to learn with him. They pooled their dreams and started to recognize possible patterns. One collective dream was improving their service to their clients. So they decided as a group to create mysteries and actions around the concept of better service. Since Camilo was the manager, his own learning had to do with the management of the overall service. His dream was to "Improve my management skills and knowledge so that I can support my staff in giving better service to our clients."

Camilo then considered actions and kinds of evidence. He developed a questionnaire for the office's clients. This revealed a host of shortcomings that he and his workers hadn't recognized. These discrepancies fueled the creation of mysteries: Why were clients feeling this way? Were they right? Initially, he had to work on motivating his own subordinates to change their attitudes and routines toward thinking more about their clients. Soon he set up training to improve communication patterns with the clients. After a few weeks he began to question whether his workers were truly committed to change and improvement. Participation began to wane in meetings. Some other workers failed to follow through on some agreed-upon changes.

NAME *Camilo Fernandez*   **OFFICE** *Sales Department*

DREAM
Improve my management skills and knowledge so that I can support my staff in giving better service to our clients.

MYSTERIES
- *What do I believe about good management?*
- *How do our clients and staff feel about the service?*
- *What do they believe is good service?*
- *How motivated are we to give the service?*
- *How do I feel placing myself in a vulnerable position towards my staff?*
- *How can I improve my communication skills?*
- *What does my office need logistically to provide good service?*
- *How can I assist my staff to understand the clients better?*
- *How to organize better the purchasing process?*
- *What do I know about my clients?*
- *How to achieve client satisfaction?*
- *How can I assimilate the feedback received so that I become a better manager?*

ACTIONS
- *Give out a questionnaire to know the feelings of clients and staff.*
- *Meet with my staff to figure out how they perceive me as a boss.*
- *Share and get feedback from my boss.*
- *Find out new ideas with respect to servicing clients.*
- *Observe the logistical functioning of my office.*

EVIDENCE
- *Opinions of customers and staff.*
- *Observations of how the services are given and what I do about it.*

Pondering why, he recognized that it was difficult to motivate others if they didn't see him changing, too. He needed to make his learning more public.

Through attending further project workshops, he found out about a lens that the research group had been developing: the Manager as a Maestro (see chapter 2). With some other managers, he examined writings about the lens and found that the most important thing for him to consider at that point was to set an example. A maestro was someone who could model learning in the organization. Therefore, he began improving how he demonstrated his own motivation and growth to his office workers. Reflecting on his prior behavior, he saw that, when faced with his clients' feedback, he would publicly say things like, "They come here for things and we have to provide them with those things. We don't need to get fancy with our communication." In retrospect, this shocked him. He had never considered that good service might depend on good communication strategies, viewing it more as a mechanical matter. One mystery then became: How do I improve my own communication skills so that I become an example to my staff? Through learning side-by-side with his workers, altering how he reacted to feedback in front of his staff, he felt their motivation turn around.

Camilo then examined another mystery: Giving better service to clients meant knowing about client satisfaction. How could he accomplish this? He began his inquiry by recognizing that his own staff was one of his immediate clients and that he really didn't know how they felt as individuals and as office team. He planned a set of actions to find out. He met for two hours with his workers and asked them, "How do you perceive me as your boss?" They wrote their answers privately and then he invited them to share their perceptions frankly. He found out that some felt they were not being challenged enough, that they could do more and better things but were limited by what the organization actually demanded of them.

He soon returned to his own boss and their concerns. His boss asked, "What changes can you think of to make work more challenging for your staff?" It was a difficult question to answer. Camilo certainly had never asked such a thing for himself. He considered his options but didn't really know about what was being done in other kinds of organizations. He remembered that one of his best friends was a very successful manager in a bank nearby. He went to visit and asked him for some tips. His friend offered some ideas and suggested reading a simple and interesting book about management that might help.

Finally, Camilo thought about how to better use his resources toward more satisfied clients. Realizing that better service depended on better teamwork, he decided not to try to solve the problem himself. He risked giving his staff the data he had and asked them to help him think of a plan. Thus he sought to support a culture of trust, honesty and respect.

The evidence Camilo collected over the weeks was exciting. Camilo was feeling much more active, his enthusiasm renewed. He saw himself working in a more collaborative and less authoritarian manner. His workers had been able to generate concrete proposals for reshaping parts of the office process. There were clear signs of a shift towards a new culture of management. Dreams, mysteries, actions and evidence had given him an organizing language to better integrate his own learning and the learning of his office workers into their professional activities.

Action Projects

Camilo's story illustrates how well-chosen words— such as dreams, mysteries, actions and evidence—can help to ignite a rich process of learning at work. However, Camilo also had a process of inquiry. Several carefully considered steps and stages organized his learning. Researchers who worked closely with managers like Camilo offered a variety of tools to help them organize their inquiry. Managers' testimony revealed that the most influential tool that supported their inquiry was the *action project*.

Several months into the La Tadeo work, the researchers formally developed the strategy of action projects. As noted earlier, after half a year of work organized around the lenses of care, generative life and symbolic conduct, the researchers noted that few managers spontaneously transferred new ideas into their practice. Many seemed stuck or content just talking about the ideas. Putting the ideas into action was not automatic. To remedy this, the researchers developed and introduced action projects.

Action projects were personal or group projects that built understanding through inquiry and practical improvements. Based on the quartet of dreams, mysteries, actions and evidence, action projects became the path through which managers got into action.

Action projects involved three essential ideas. First, they asked managers to engage in personally meaningful and focused inquiry centered on bettering their practice. Second, they invited managers to collaborate within a critical but supportive group throughout their inquiry. And third, they guided managers through cycles of actions and reflections. Since action projects emerged as a central and robust strategy in fostering understanding in action, we will expand on these features in the following sub-sections.

Personal Commitment to Change

Personal commitment to change was an important ingredient in action projects. The approach encouraged such investment by asking participants, individually or in small groups, to invent alternatives and select action projects of genuine importance to them. One project survey showed that all the managers (100%) listed their personal commitment to change as the criterion that most helped them in action projects. This suggested that those who engaged successfully in action projects truly wanted to improve. These managers also tended to believe that such a change would not happen overnight. Learning would develop incrementally over time. The managers also believed that they could help others grow through collaborative work arrangements and through sharing their experiences of inquiry. Being a lone maverick was not a good strategy.

Personal commitment meant that managers owned their dreams and mysteries—even if these were collaboratively generated with a group of colleagues or the organization writ large. To be workable, it also meant that the action project needed to lie within a manager's sphere of influence: the manager could do what needed to be done through personal efforts and marshalling subordinates and colleagues. For example, questions such as "What actions do I make that help or hinder a meeting?" "How can I learn how other offices handle this issue?" or "What other models or strategies can I use to help me manage my time better?" addressed the personal development of managers' practice and were well within the bounds of their control. Such questions were open-ended enough to allow for rich exploration and growth.

Critical and Supportive Group

Even if managers chose very personal and individual dreams and mysteries for their action project, they never engaged in the inquiry process alone. Managers worked collaboratively in small groups as they made plans, gave updates on progress, and collected suggestions on how to deepen their inquiry. These groups sometimes included managers from a single office and sometimes across offices. Occasionally a small group of managers created a shared action project. Though such support groups varied in size throughout the final years of the project, they typically included about three to four colleagues and, from time to time, a researcher who facilitated conversations and feedback. Often, as in the opening example of the three Friday meetings, managers shared their inquiry plans and progress with the larger group for feedback.

Cycles of Action and Reflection

Finally, action projects contained clear cycles of acting and reflecting. Action and reflection fueled each other, since actions produced information for reflection and reflection, in turn, produced new insights and ideas that led people back into action. Although action projects ranged in scale—early on most action projects were four to six weeks in length while later some action projects unfolded over a full year—some general guidelines informed the general style of actions and reflections. The following criteria helped to ensure that actions revealed and deepened managers' understanding, as well as advancing practical ends. In workshops early in the project, the researchers presented these criteria to the managers, who, in turn, practiced designing appropriate actions:

- *Intentional*: The managers were encouraged to plan their actions thoughtfully in advance, with a clear rationale. Though some actions might emerge from circumstances, in general it's worth acting intentionally over time while advancing toward a particular goal.
- *Informed*: The managers tried to design their actions using as much information as was available. Serious actions were not to be taken on a whim or in the face of information advising to the contrary. When possible, managers would draw on multiple sources of information.
- *Creative*: The best actions were somewhat challenging, with unpredictable outcomes, not simple, rote or

mechanical. It was important for the managers to push themselves, to move in new directions, and to take reasonable risks.

- *Flexible*: Actions were designed to allow real-time adjustments in the context of work, but eschew tendencies some managers had for total improvisation.
- *Generative*: Actions were chosen to generate new information, perspectives and knowledge in a variety of forms around the central questions, topics, and goals of inquiry.
- *Documentable*: Built into the actions themselves were techniques of gathering and recording information. A variety of means—notes, reflections written shortly afterward, tape recording, videotaping, and so on—helped to capture valuable data.

Married to managers' actions was the vital counterpart of reflection. To help organize the reflective process in action projects, participants bore in mind the following basic—but certainly not rigid—principles:

- *Analysis:* After a round of action, managers examined their new information to make sense of it, looking for trends, themes, categories, rationales, and so on. After and sometimes during periods of analysis, managers connected their new information and insights back to their dreams and mysteries.
- *Feedback*: The managers, other members of their work groups, and the facilitators worked together to provide critical but supportive feedback. Usually everyone critiqued and probed the actions and evidence. They discussed issues of subjectivity and bias, and offer suggestions and perspectives for future actions. Although it took some time to master this style of feedback, many participants soon learned to ask constructive questions such as, "Why did you do that?" "Why did you think that?" "Have you considered this?"

- *Adjustments:* With the feedback from the work group, managers then developed plans for the next round of actions. Typically, managers worked closely with the facilitators to make final adjustments to their plans before entering the next cycle of actions.

During one-on-one or larger meetings, the researchers worked with the managers on these criteria. The researchers developed checklists and guidelines that managers could use to keep track of the criteria. One such checklist appears on the following page.

Stages of Action Projects

Many interesting trends emerged as groups of managers began implementing their action projects. For one, the action projects showed signs of some natural key stages. For example, Hernando, an electrical engineer at La Tadeo, started his action project by articulating his dreams and mysteries. He wanted to find a way of reducing high costs that reflected poor electric use and wiring in much of the equipment used in the university laboratories. His initial actions focused on finding alternatives that existed, considering different types of breakers and visiting suppliers to check new technologies. Hernando bought some books, asked advice from friends, and looked at different models. After exploring and gathering information, Hernando began to find some ways to cut electric costs at La Tadeo. He focused in on three or four key strategies and refined them over a few weeks. When at last he felt that he had gathered enough information and evidence about the viability of his project, he wrote up a memo to share with his supervisor. The supervisor was so impressed with the projected savings to the organization that he invited Hernando to give a series of presentations to colleagues and organization supervisors, who began to adopt his recommendations.

As in Hernando's case, many action projects naturally fell into some basic stages in keeping with the general idea of action research: *planning, exploration, focused inquiry,* and *synthesis.* These stages were not discrete. At times, they overlapped and combined. Though many

Action Project Checklist		Not Really	Some-what	Abso-lutely!
I. To what degree are you engaged in *personally meaningful* **and** *focused inquiry* **centered on** *bettering your practice?*	To what degree are you personally committed to changing your practice?			
	To what degree are you doing inquiry around an area you truly believe is important to you and is under your control?			
	To what degree have you phrased questions and are engaging in inquiry around your actions?			
II. To what degree are you *collaborating* **within a** *critical, supportive group* **throughout your** *inquiry?*	To what degree are you collaboratively working with 1–4 colleagues to critique and support each other's inquiry?			
	To what degree are you working with a facilitator?			
	To what degree are you presenting your inquiry to the larger group in the organization?			
III. To what degree are you *articulating* **and** *engaging in cycles of inquiry-oriented actions and reflections?*	To what degree are your actions			
	... intentional?			
	... informed?			
	... creative?			
	... flexible?			
	... generative?			
	... documentable?			
	To what degree do your reflections have moments of			
	... analysis?			
	... feedback?			
	... adjustments?			

managers were not aware of such stages, the researchers observed them and occasionally helped managers make transitions from one stage to the next. It's worth bearing them in mind when facilitating action projects in any setting.

Planning

In this stage, managers began the process by creating personally and professionally relevant dreams and mysteries: What did they really want to work on in their practice? Some managers commenced this step alone while others processed their reflections more publicly in small groups. In either case, managers created questions and visions that were clear, personally meaningful, central to their practice, focused on actions under their control, and that contributed to the organization's knowledge. Though some managers seemed already to have such dreams and mysteries before ever encountering the idea of action projects, many did not, and explored and experimented a bit before they settled on a particular theme.

Using the criteria presented earlier for actions and reflections, managers then created sequences of actions and ways of gathering evidence to advance their dreams and understand their mysteries. They wrote down these plans and often shared them for feedback.

Exploration

Many managers' action projects then gave way to an exploratory stage. In it, managers carried out initial actions, reflected, and gathered evidence that explored the territory of inquiry in divergent ways. Hernando's reading books, experimenting with different electrical configurations, and talking with friends all were good examples of explorative actions. The researchers encouraged the managers to gather information using combinations of techniques: personal journals, interviews, written reflections, video or tape recorders and

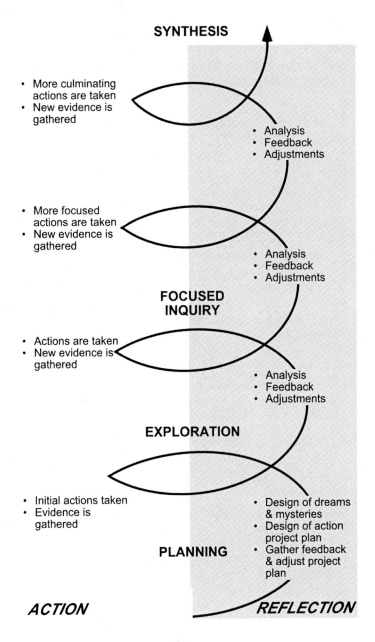

SYNTHESIS

- More culminating actions are taken
- New evidence is gathered

- Analysis
- Feedback
- Adjustments

- More focused actions are taken
- New evidence is gathered

- Analysis
- Feedback
- Adjustments

FOCUSED INQUIRY

- Actions are taken
- New evidence is gathered

- Analysis
- Feedback
- Adjustments

EXPLORATION

- Initial actions taken
- Evidence is gathered

- Design of dreams & mysteries
- Design of action project plan
- Gather feedback & adjust project plan

PLANNING

ACTION

REFLECTION

observations from others. Alone and collaboratively within their small work groups, the managers analyzed their information and mapped their insights in relation to their dreams and mysteries.

Focused Inquiry

Characteristically, the stage of exploration led to a stage of focused inquiry. The managers began to carry out more systematically focused actions and evidence to match. The managers created models, categories, checklists or other tools that captured, explained or helped to guide their future actions. Hernando's tests of his ideas and observations and revisions of his practice based on ideas about better electrical configurations were examples of such a focused inquiry stage.

Synthesis

Finally, most managers reached a final *synthesis stage.* They began to wrap up their actions and evidence gathering, and to coalesce and share their understandings to the wider group. They created and revised final summary products to share their conclusions, such as memos, presentations and booklets. Hernando's memo shared with his boss and his presentations to others exemplified the synthesis stage.

The spiral diagram on the following page summaries the four emergent stages of inquiry.

Findings about Integrating Learning and Work

The stories about the Friday sessions, Camilo, and Hernando show that some managers integrated learning into their work. But, looking at the larger pool of participants, what impact did work as inquiry, action projects and the Compass of Inquiry have on the organization and the individuals? What helped and hindered the managers as they tried to integrate learning into their work?

To understand better how the strategies outlined in this chapter impacted the managers and their culture, the researchers adopted a general action research methodology in which they worked closely with the managers, documented their development, conducted participant interviews and qualitative and quantitative impact surveys. Since the method drew on participants' perspectives, the data is certainly susceptible to positive bias. Though methods of triangulation were used, checking results through multiple sources, the findings should be viewed with caution.

Impact of Integrating Learning in Work

In general the data suggest that the approach assisted managers in better integrating learning into work. The italics that appear are the words that correspond directly to interview or questionnaire items. In general, almost all the managers reported that action projects were key for learning in their work *because they set up the structure of action-reflection.* They also noted that action projects *created a climate of sharing based on tangible products.* Although action projects had many supporters, the researchers found it was *difficult for some managers to view action projects as part of— not separate from — their regular work.*

The researchers were able to assess impact within two different sets of managers: the *classics*—those who had been in the project from the beginning—and the *new managers*—those who joined later and became acquainted with the ideas through special workshops built on the experience to that point.

The Classic Managers noted that integrating learning into their work yielded *better understanding of and relations with others (95.5% reporting this), better overall communication skills (95.5%), more positive attitudes (90.9%), personal satisfaction (86.4%)* and a *better quality of work (86.4%).* Organizationally, they reported that the approach led to a stronger focus on *serving the internal* clients (77.2%), better productivity (72.3%) and *solving problems (72.2%)*. Other reflections revealed that many managers sensed a culture change toward *more valuing of the managers, who they are and how they feel*. However, the managers also reported that the organizational impact was not as apparent or strong as the individual impact. Still, they perceived that, in offices that were using work as inquiry, action projects, and the Compass, ideas were *changing the micro-cultures, becoming more respectful* and *human centered*.

The individual impact on the new managers was measured using pre- and post-surveys and written reflections. Analysis revealed that a focus on integrating learning in work contributed to strong shifts in how managers viewed their work strategies. For example, over 85% of the managers noted increases in *the quality of personal reflection strategies*, increases in *the quality of strategies to manage conflicts*, increases in *the quality of strategies for creating more personal meaning in their work*, better *giving and receiving feedback*, and improved strategies for *motivating others and creating better products/services*.

Although these findings suggest a highly positive impact, we are quick to point out that all was indeed not so idyllic. The next section will outline what may have facilitated these positive outcomes as well as share some specific problems.

What Helped or Hindered

In surveys and focus group interviews, the managers noted the following factors as strongly assisting them in integrating learning into their work: the *researcher/group facilitators (100%)*, their *personal/professional will and interests (100%)*, *Self Reflections (100%)*, *the ability to give/ receive feedback (95.5%)*, the *Inquiry Lenses (Care, Symbolic Conduct, Generative Life) (90.8%)*, the *Friday meetings (90.9%)*, *the PZ External Group (90.9%)*, and *cycles of action-reflection (90.9%)*.

The Compass of Inquiry also was often cited as useful in interviews. They reported that the language was intuitive, easy to remember, inspirational and easy to explain to others. All of these criteria worked nicely to close the idea-action gap.

But all was not rosy. Throughout the project, the managers also reported many obstacles to integrating learning and work. Though not in as striking numbers, the managers noted that the major challenges to this approach at La Tadeo were *lack of free time (50%), organizational structures and bureaucracy (27%)* and *cultural habits (aggressiveness, tardiness, interrupting, etc.) (27%)*.

The managers reported in interviews the struggle to keep their projects within their sphere of control. Although the researchers emphasized this criterion, some managers continued to attempt action projects that focused on changing the practices of others, not their own. Another challenge appeared for the managers who worked under bosses who did not support action projects. These managers felt that they were playing by two sets of rules. Some managers commented that they felt that their action projects needed to be covert, not revealed to their immediate unsupportive boss. More often than not, such action projects faltered. Finally, managers who could not find a way to connect their action projects into their daily routines struggled. Those managers who created action projects that fell outside the natural daily workflow seemed to advance slower than those managers who chose topics and questions that directly connected.

Where the Impact Fell

As mentioned earlier, the results should be viewed as an overestimate of impact, given the likely positive bias in the responses of people. However, the findings do suggest that integrating learning into work using a core value of work as inquiry, a language of dreams, mysteries, actions, and evidence, and the structure of action projects had a positive impact on how managers at La Tadeo felt and how they related to others in their work. Recalling the *bottom lines* introduced in chapter 2, the approach did much to advance humanistic bottom lines.

However, the choices that managers made for their action projects generally did not attend as much to the operational and productive platforms. This was especially so for the classic managers. The new managers showed an increase in attention to the operational and productivity bottom lines, although attention to humanistic bottom lines still dominated. Since the method applies equally well in principle to all three, we interpret this as a reflection of our particular emphasis and timing. The project's historical focus intentionally fell on the individual learning and meaning making of the managers. Moreover, an early orientation to the humanistic dimension may be natural. Organizational theorist Peter Senge suggests that humanistic gains tend to emerge first in interventions focused on organizational learning, followed by operational and productive benefits.

In any case, work as inquiry, action projects and the language are no panacea. True, they provide steps towards creating a culture that values the integration of learning in work. Such steps give shape to how people interact for understanding. But how can these interactions, these new patterns of collaboration be sustained? The next chapter will examine in more detail a vital area in creating organizational understanding in action: Smart Cultures of Communication.

Reflection

Reflect on a project you attempted in the past, applying the spiral of action and reflection or the Compass of Inquiry. Can you use these tools to describe what you did or tried to do in an illuminating way?

What aspects of your work do you think would have good potential for inquiry?

With those aspects in mind, what are your most important dreams and mysteries?

What are the main challenges you might face in planning and developing meaningful action projects?

Action

When you receive a request or order to do something, stop and think: How can you link the way you proceed to your personal or organizational dreams?

Choose a very small scale action project to get started—something you can do with a little effort in a day or a few days. Do it! (It's best to start small.)

4. Smart Cultures of Communication

Wednesday's Ritual

"Ok, folks, let's begin," said Julia, a twenty year veteran administrator within La Tadeo.

Over coffee and donuts, she and eight of her staff gathered for their new weekly ritual: Wednesday Updates and Office Evaluation. The agenda for the day included office feedback. During the preceding weeks, the staff had gathered evaluations from the office's clients—other people at La Tadeo—about their office performance. In this meeting, the group would look over the results of the surveys.

As they examined the data, Julia invited each staff member to offer opinions of the office's strengths and weaknesses. People around the table took notes, listened, and asked each other questions to clarify points. Many staff members advanced suggestions about how to better monitor and enhance the office performance. The brainstorming ended with the group planning concrete action projects (see chapter 3), with various staff members volunteering as action project leaders.

"It hasn't always been like this," commented Juan Ricardo, one of the workers, after the meeting. "We used to meet every now and then but it was unorganized. We didn't have an agenda. People talked about whatever popped into their heads and went on and on. Nobody ever asked me for my opinions or really listened to me.

We were just told what to do. I think this is first time that I feel recognized as a human being here, with good ideas toward improving our work." Many others shared similar feelings.

Such experiences raise questions about how people can better come together and communicate for understanding. Earlier chapters noted a central challenge in organizational understanding: creating and sustaining cultures that support learning. Concepts such as *work as inquiry, action projects* and the *bottom lines* suggest that organizational understanding depends on cultures that put a premium on reflection, action, and feedback, and make people feel safe to try out new ideas and sometimes fail. If such practices are to succeed, people must communicate well—as they were in Julia's meetings. Accordingly, this chapter introduces the idea of smart cultures of communication. It introduces and illustrates three culture-making tools from the work at La Tadeo. The chapter concludes with lessons the researchers learned about how best to bridge the idea-action gap when trying to create such cultures.

Not Just Nice, But Smart

Through working with offices like Julia's, the researchers witnessed the crucial role basic communication practices played in cultivating understanding in action. The people that moved their action projects forward effectively also interacted in particular ways. Like Julia and Juan Ricardo, they listened well, asked questions, and gave each other constructive feedback. In contrast, managers who struggled with their action projects seemed to lack such communication strategies. They often interrupted or ignored each other. They did not solicit each other's ideas or ask for feedback. They argued endlessly and criticized sharply, escalating conflicts. It became clear that different offices had different micro-cultures of communication that affected group and individual understandings. These micro-cultures made it easier for some offices to adopt and develop practices of understanding in action.

The literature is replete with a variety of definitions of communication. For the project's purposes, communication meant the manner in which people shared, built, made meaning out of and interacted with information. When the researchers assessed Julia and her colleague's culture of communication, they examined the beliefs and practices that shaped how they exchanged ideas, listened to the ideas of others, encouraged others to contribute opinions, constructed shared understanding and consensus, and evaluated options.

At first blush, such a culture of communication might simply feel nice, polite, and even democratic. Certainly it is. However, it is much, much more. Such a culture is not just nice, *it is also smart.* It is a smart culture of communication because it is driven by beliefs and actions that engage people in generating ideas, gathering information, exchanging opinions, evaluating perspectives, integrating various points of view, and informing future actions. These smart strategies worked to improve individual, group and organization understanding in action. In her Wednesday office meetings, Julia was creating a smarter culture that reinforced the importance of intelligent communication. Moreover, people like Juan Ricardo were beginning to think and act differently.

However, as mentioned earlier, many offices in the university did not have such smart cultures. Actions would pass by without feedback and mistakes would be repeated. Managers had few strategies for soliciting and gathering new ideas. People would often interrupt, argue, or occasionally threaten each other. Issues became polarized, employees became defensive and cynical. Offices argued over jurisdiction and territoriality. In such places it was difficult to advance action projects.

Accordingly, the investigative team worked closely with the managers to promote smarter cultures of communication. In keeping with the theme from chapter 1 of tools as culture makers, the investigators hypothesized that groups could gain much from communication tools that the leader could use, model and message within a group. Throughout the research of the project, this assumption proved correct and investigators dedicated much energy in crafting tools that worked well in the university management context.

Some of these tools emerged from patterns of practice among successful managers. The researchers observed managers in action and noted how they dealt with others. Through weekly reflections with these managers, the researchers developed tools that reflected good practice. Other tools drew upon the researchers' personal experience and on literature about how to better share ideas, brainstorm, and ask questions. All tools aimed to help managers think differently and augment the quality of the interactions in their office.

In this chapter, we will introduce three smart tools for a culture of communication: *Generative Conversations*, the *Ladder of Feedback*, and *Healthy Corridor Talk*. Though these three tools had different levels of presence in the project, the authors believe that they provide building blocks with which offices and organizations can build smarter cultures of communication. After discussion of the three tools, a final section describes the impact of and lessons from this approach.

Generative Conversations

"Rosa, do you have a second?" said Oscar as he passed her in the hallway.

"Uh, well," she said glancing at her watch. "Sure, shoot."

"I have the solution to cutting costs. I looked at the figures on the employee reports and realized we could save a bundle by reducing all these part-timers. You know, we continually have to train new part-time employees since they don't stay very long."

"And let me guess," sighed Rosa, "your idea is to hire full-timers to take over?"

"Well, yeah." Oscar stumbled.

"Look, I know you are still new here so I will put it simply: It won't work because full-timers mean more health insurance costs. And besides, you shouldn't even be reading those reports."

"Thanks for putting it simply," Oscar scoffed. "But listen for a second and you'll see that I thought of that already. And you gave me those reports last week to…"

"Oh, don't get smart with me. I listen plenty!" Rosa interrupted, raising her voice. "Like last time when you brought me that genius idea about changing phone companies. What a fiasco that was." She waved her arm in the air. "You're lucky to still be here!"

Conversations like this happened all too often among the administration at La Tadeo—an idea worth responding, a sharply skeptical response, rising anger, and a downspiral into misunderstandings and sometimes threats. Clearly, such conversations reflect the very opposite of a smart culture of communication. Instead, a smart culture promotes what the researchers observed and called *Generative Conversations,* avoiding degenerative conversations like the one above.

Generative Conversations are interactions that support learning, inquiry, and growth. They do this through a smooth exchange of information, collaboratively building ideas and giving and receiving thoughtful many-sided feedback to inform actions. In contrast, degenerative conversations inhibit learning and inquiry through poor information exchange, lack of collective idea building and escalating defensiveness.

The investigators worked with the university managers by observing the generative and de-generative moves managers made in informal conversations and meetings. The investigators noted what appeared to be positive and negative patterns and then checked this out with the managers. As important moves accumulated, the researchers developed a guiding tool that other managers could use to learn to foster a smart culture of communication. The researchers and managers introduced this tool in the Encuentros, mini-courses that participants took to better understand the ideas (see chapter 6 for further details). The tool described five conversational moves that promoted Generative Conversations and five that provoked degenerative ones. The five positive moves were:

Clarifying

When someone took an action or proposed an idea that needed a response, colleagues would thoughtfully consider it and pose questions to make unclear points clearer. For example, a secretary might repeat back what she heard her boss say to check its meaning. A colleague might ask another to explain what she meant by a particular word or phrase. In a meeting, a worker might ask questions about parts of a plan that seemed unclear. In general, clarifying aimed at gathering more information about an action idea prior to offering reactions.

Probing

When people interacted, sometimes they asked questions that elicited implicit assumptions, criteria and underlying goals. A worker might say, "Gosh, this office really is a horrible place to work." To which a colleague might respond by probing with, "What makes you say that?" or "What are some other offices like?" Such questions sought to unpack conclusions, check meanings, and reveal criteria, assumptions and goals. Probing was a fundamental move in Generative Conversations since it created a climate of inquiry and learning among colleagues.

Testing

The researchers noted that managers sometimes would offer and test their ideas and actions for open public feedback and conversation. Such a practice matches a central recommendation of organizational theorists Chris Argyris and Donald Schön for organizational learning. For example, an office director and a superior might meet to plan next year's budget. The director might test his or her understanding of the department's goals by asking, "I think the goals for next year are . . . is that on target or do you see it differently?" Alternatively, in an office meeting a worker might test an idea by saying, "My sense is that people might like more time to think about solutions before discussing them now. Is that right?" Both examples illustrate how testing invited input by presenting an understanding as partial and open to reconstruction.

Openness

It was tremendously helpful when people welcomed feedback, discussion, probing, or critique. For example, a boss might bring up a new idea with some colleagues, say, "And I'd be very interested in what you all think about it," and then conduct a pro-and-con discussion without defensiveness. Or perhaps two workers would pass in the hallway, one saying to the other, "I'd really like to talk to you about that new contract procedure you designed, some really nice aspects and a couple of puzzles." The other would welcome the feedback by saying, "Yes, of course. I'd like to hear how it is working. When could we meet?" Such openness was a challenge to attain when managers did not solicit feedback, but it remained an important move in conducting Generative Conversations.

Constructing

With many ideas often on the table, it was helpful when people compared, connected, and integrated these ideas. For example, three people in a meeting presented solutions to a problem. One participant might initiate a process of pro-ing and con-ing all three systematically and comparatively to build a shared view of the options. Or a small group might have a conversation in the hallway, each person making regular references to what the others had said: "When you said that, it makes me think..." or "Your idea seems very related to what I think she is saying." Constructing connections and contrasts played a crucial role in Generative Conversations because it fostered a shared understanding and coherent plans of action.

As mentioned earlier, the investigators also observed many conversations that were far from ideal. Many were de-generative rather than generative. As noted earlier, degenerative conversations inhibited learning and inquiry and escalated toward conflict. Besides describing positive moves, the communications tool introduced to managers also characterized five negative moves to avoid:

Dismissing

Sometimes people responded to others' ideas or actions in dismissive ways that did not give them a genuine hearing. For example, when a worker shared her thinking about organizing interoffice memos better, a colleague would dismiss it by remaining silent or only offering superficial comments such as, "Yeah," "Interesting," or "Neat." Often, dismissive colleagues would also change the topic or ignore the idea altogether: "Hmmm, interesting. You know, I wanted to check with you about..."

Dismissive behaviors often included assuming consensus about not pursuing an idea. For example, if a participant in a meeting sketched a better way to schedule purchases, someone might say, "Well, we all think that is a good idea of course. However, we would have to work it out with the accounting office, and we all know what a mess that would be. So what next?" Dismissive conversational moves sent messages that inquiry was not paramount and typically led to misunderstandings and bad feelings.

Asserting

When people stated ideas, information, and opinions as truths or "the only way," it became difficult for colleagues to probe or critique. For example, a manager might say, "The only way to fix it is..." or "The reality is..." Assertive moves created adversarial relationships, destroyed empathy, and reinforced narrow and inflexible patterns of communication.

Defensiveness

When managers discussed or critiqued someone's ideas or actions, often times the person assumed an excessively closed and threatened posture. For example, when a colleague raised an idea and others began to ask questions to clarify it or probe its viability, the person might become flustered, angry, and uncooperative.

Negative Critique

When managers discussed ideas or actions, critical comments, lists of pitfalls, and upbraiding often dominated the conversation. For example, in an office meeting, a manager presented an idea about how the office might better keep track of its purchase orders. Many colleagues immediately attacked her idea. People interrupted her saying what they didn't like about it and why it wouldn't work. Indeed, perhaps the idea was not so good. However, such sweeping negative reactions are likely to reject good ideas prematurely, miss the opportunity to improve mixed ideas, discourage people from offering ideas at all, and generate ill feelings and alienation.

Isolating

A Generative Conversation became difficult to sustain when participants made little or no effort to connect ideas, acknowledge others' positions, compare, contrast, pro-con or weave information together. For example, if two solutions to a problem arose over lunch, the discussants might simply say which one they liked with no conversation about why. If they disagreed on an approach, they would make no effort to find a compromise or create a third shared solution.

As these categories make apparent, Generative Conversations and their opposite have much to do with the three lenses introduced in chapter 2. Generative Conversations display good symbolic conduct with caring side-messages in keeping with a generative life. In contrast, degenerative conversations send negative signals with their symbolic conduct, displaying lack of care and neglect of a generative life. Conversation, in short, is a powerful locus of culture-making, and a tool like Generative Conversations is an important culture-maker and a way of integrating work and learning, the second and third themes of Understanding for Organizations.

In order to cultivate Generative Conversations and avoid degenerative ones, the researchers presented the following reflection sheet to managers. Managers rated their behavior and discussed in small groups why they acted differently in different situations. This reflection sheet was so useful to some managers that they began to use it with their office personnel before and after office meetings. Although the sheet asked people to rate themselves on a quantitative Likert scale, the managers did not collect the ratings. Rather, the goal was to stimulate a personal and group reflection on the conversational moves that supported or inhibited smart cultures of communication.

Generative Conversations Reflection Sheet

	Description	Never		Some-times		Always
CLARIFY	I thoughtfully consider others' ideas and/or actions and pose questions to make unclear points clearer. *Examples:* "*I am not quite clear, can you say more about X?*" "*What was the differences between Y and Z?*" etc.	1	2	3	4	5
PROBE	I thoughtfully probe people's ideas and/or actions for their assumptions, underlying goals, and possible remedies. *Examples:* "*What makes you think that?*" "*When you did X, what were your goals?*" "*Do you have ideas or suggestions about that?*" etc.	1	2	3	4	5
TEST	I offer and solicit feedback and conversation around perceptions that I hold about ideas and/or actions. *Examples:* "*I think the problem is X. How do others see this?*" "*Some options might be A, B or C. What do people think about these?*" etc.	1	2	3	4	5
BE OPEN	I openly welcome discussion, critique and feedback from different perspectives about ideas and/or actions. *Examples:* "*Thanks for that idea, it's very helpful.*" "*That's good advice.*" "*I hear what you are saying, I'll need to think about that more.*" etc.	1	2	3	4	5
BUILD IDEAS	In groups I publicly acknowledge, compare, integrate and/or build ideas with others about ideas and/or actions. *Examples:* "*I hear you saying A and she saying B, maybe we can put them together to make C?*" "*That connects very well to what he said earlier.*" "*Relating to what you said earlier …*" etc.	1	2	3	4	5
DISMISS	I do not thoughtfully consider, reflect on, value or respond to others' ideas and/or actions. I assume consensus and/or do not publicly test or investigate people's ideas and/or actions since I view their assumptions are not necessary or important. *Examples:* "*That is simply not important to discuss*" "*That does not relate*" "*We can't talk about that now*" "*Yes we all like your idea. Now let's move on.*" etc.	1	2	3	4	5
ASSERT	I present and advocate my ideas and/or actions as truths and as the "only way" which are not open for thoughtful discussion, probing or critique. *Examples:* "*The problem is X.*" "*The answer is Y.*" "*What we have to do is Z.*"	1	2	3	4	5
ACT DEFENSIVELY	When others attempt to thoughtfully discuss, probe or critique my ideas and/or actions, I get angry, frustrated, feel attacked and generally defensive. When others levy criticism around my ideas and/or actions, I make retaliating remarks and/or personal attacks that heighten the tension.	1	2	3	4	5
REACT NEGATIVELY	I aggressively critique others' ideas and/or actions only from a negative perspective. *Examples:* "*Why your idea won't work is …*" "*The problem is …*" "*What you haven't taken into account is …*" "*What I don't like is …*" etc.	1	2	3	4	5
LEAVE IDEAS DISCONNECTED	I do not thread others' comments together, connect ideas to what others have mentioned, or make no effort to craft shared understandings of others' ideas and/or actions for my or the group's benefit.	1	2	3	4	5

The Ladder of Feedback

Valencia, a Project Zero researcher, worked closely with Arturo, a high level La Tadeo manager. Arturo often told Valencia that he wanted to improve the way he interacted with his staff. Valencia observed and participated in many meetings with Arturo and his staff. In meetings, Arturo and his staff frequently offered harsh critiques and rejected someone's ideas immediately. When others gave feedback, the recipient often became defensive. People generally did not incorporate ideas or feedback into future actions.

Valencia concluded that people had never learned to how to give feedback thoughtfully. To remedy this, the researchers worked with Arturo and other managers to introduce a specific tool for feedback situations, which came to be called The Ladder of Feedback. The managers became acquainted with the Ladder through the workshop meetings and the Encuentros (see chapter 6) and began to use the Ladder in their office meetings.

The Ladder had four intuitive (but not so simple) steps: first *Clarify* with questions, then *Value* the positive features, then offer *Concerns*, and finally *Suggest* next steps. These steps have obvious connections to the Generative Conversations tool. Indeed, both tools attempt to shape interactions in more constructive ways. However, The Ladder of Feedback was specialized, providing a systematic and thoughtful template for feedback. With that in mind, let us examine each step of the Ladder.

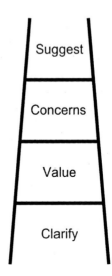

Clarify

When a manager put an idea on the table, others often would respond critically to what they thought the idea was without really understanding it.

Clarifying with questions about unclear points or absent elements before giving feedback ensured that the idea discussed was the idea intended. For example, suppose a manager sketched a new policy about how to track office purchases. The manager might then ask for questions of clarification. The others might pose questions like, "When would this take effect?" "What is the current policy exactly?" "What qualifies as a purchase?"

As noted, applying the Ladder provide trickier than it might seem. The researchers discovered that participants often quite spontaneously would ask questions of clarification that were little more than negative reactions, for instance, "How could we possibly get this new tracking scheme ready in time?" or "Why do you think there's anything at all wrong with the current policy?" To use the Ladder well, participants had to discipline themselves to ask genuine questions of clarification like the examples listed above, resisting the impulse simply to translate their skepticism into question form.

Value

Beyond clarification, *valuing* people and their ideas was important. All too often, people tended to jump to their critiques without identifying positive points. In contrast, valuing helped to create a supportive environment of inquiry. To continue the example of the purchasing policy, the manager who presented the plan might ask, "Okay, what do you like about this idea?" Participants would explicitly state what they saw as the positive points: "I see how this proposal might better work to control costs" or "I really like the idea of creating a shared policy rather than the current scatter." Valuing helped to establish a supportive climate. But valuing was not just a matter of being nice. Valuing was informative as well, indicating what was good about an idea, so that if the idea were altered, the new version could retain its positive features.

Here again, participants not uncommonly fell into a trap, valuing in a token way and briskly proceeding to their concerns. A participant might say, for example, "Great idea, although I'm concerned about…" or "I think this could make a real difference, but…" Good use of the Ladder demanded inhibiting the impulse to breeze past the valuing stage.

Concerns

Naturally, there were often legitimate concerns with an idea. After clarification and valuing was the time to raise them—not as derisive accusations or abrasive criticisms, but as honest thoughts and information. For example, in the case of the purchasing policy, someone might say, "A concern I have is who will oversee this policy—everyone seems to be pretty busy as is," or "I worry about whether this policy will make others feel overburdened with more rules and procedures."

Suggest

However well phrased, concerns were often a sensitive point. Accordingly, offering constructive *suggestions* became the last vital rung. For example, a participant in the office purchasing scenario might say, "I would suggest asking someone if they want to be responsible for overseeing this policy, or perhaps even asking if we could hire another person to assist us," or "Perhaps it would be worthwhile to investigate whether other offices have similar policies and how they deal with them."

Because suggestions usually connected directly to concerns the managers raised, often these two steps collapsed into one. A manager might say, "I am worried that your plan costs too much money, so maybe you could look into ways to cut costs," or "I am concerned that this plan doesn't speak to what the clients really are looking for, so perhaps you could interview some of our clients in order to be sure."

The Ladder of Feedback was perhaps the most widely applied communication tool within the Understanding for Organizations project. It was simple and easy to remember, and it produced quick results. The Ladder also fit well with the themes of care, symbolic conduct, and the generative life and helped the three groups dealing with these themes to conduct their meetings. Moreover, the Ladder connected well to the action projects. Since action projects asked for groups to meet on a weekly basis to share progress and give feedback, the Ladder provided a practical tool for organizing the feedback process. Some managers felt good enough about the Ladder to use it in their meetings with their office personnel and meetings with other managers in the organization.

Healthy Corridor Talk

Ismael and Maria Jimena exited a meeting in which they had said hardly anything. A few minutes later, they gathered as they usually did after such meetings, down a quiet hall with their coffee. Ismael leaned on the wall, rolling his eyes. "That meeting was a total waste of time. And can you believe Tomas? Does he really think that his plan is going to fly with the other offices?"

"I know," Maria Jimena agreed while sipping her coffee. "I can't imagine the chief will even let him present it. But I've heard that the chief is getting all kinds of pressure about it. And he's always protecting Tomas," she sighed. "But we tried that same idea three years ago and it flopped. Just wait until the other offices hear about it. They're going to go berserk."

"Yeah, I better let Clare know about the idea to prepare her. She'll be the first to flip out since it will affect her office directly."

Scenarios like Ismael and Maria Jimena's were prominent in the culture of communication at La Tadeo. From the early days of the project, the researchers observed that many people remained silent in meetings or even vocalized support, but gathered later in the hallways and offices to process their negative thoughts and feelings about the meeting. The practice was so common that a manager quipped, "For a one-hour meeting I bet we spend two or three hours afterward talking about what really happened and what people are really thinking." The researchers began to call this phenomena *corridor talk*.There were some understandable reasons why managers like Ismael and Maria Jimena engaged in corridor talk. Perhaps they wanted to raise a concern in private or just get something off their chest. Corridor talk also allowed people a private forum to iron out difficulties. In that sense, corridor talk can be a safe place to raise personal concerns, test ideas, get frank and informal feedback, make personal connections and build legitimate coalitions. However, when corridor talk became the main channel for processing feelings, making judgments, and exchanging information, it threatened smart cultures of communication in two important ways.

First, corridor talk contributed to system information loss. As emphasized in chapter 1, developing understanding involves gathering feedback to inform actions better. Corridor talk undermined this by channeling feedback away from public forums. This channeling led to less informed individual, group, and organizational actions. Perhaps Maria Jimena's concerns could help improve Tomas' proposal. Perhaps Ismael's worry about the reactions of the offices could encourage people to develop a strategy. We will never know.

Secondly, corridor talk bred mistrust among people and led them to make sweeping generalizations about their colleagues and organizational issues. Managers too often gathered together to spread gossip, undermine decisions, and plot against others. Like a chemical chain reaction, corridor talk spawned a culture of mistrust and misunderstanding. If any feedback eventually got back to others like Tomas or the chief, it felt sneaky. Tomas might conclude, not unreasonably, that people are talking and even scheming outside the meetings. The chief might feel that he cannot trust Maria Jimena or Ismael to be team players in the organization. Also, corridor talk promoted unchecked assumptions, mental models, and negative stereotypes about people. Maria Jimena made judgments that the chief "always protects Tomas" and "is under pressure." In the gossipy pairs and trios of typical corridor talk, sweeping generalizations of people and situations thrived.

To raise awareness of the dangers of corridor talk, the researchers introduced a reflective tool for managers. It invited managers to examine what motivates the practice of corridor talk and how they might keep it from becoming destructive. Many ideas were on the table during the initial stages of the project, and this tool did not see as much use as some of the others. Nonetheless, the authors offer to readers, since corridor talk continued to be a prominent and often pernicious phenomenon within La Tadeo.

The researchers identified seven categories that motivated corridor talk. These categories depicted the mixed nature of corridor talk: At times, it seemed to be a functional behavior for dealing with the larger system or culture. At other times, it did mischief.

Catharsis

Managers often needed to get feelings off their chest outside of the formal arena of feedback. They did this in order to feel better. Such a feeling would be a cathartic motivation for corridor talk. For example, after a meeting in which a worker publicly disagreed with a decision, he chose to discuss it with a researcher over lunch. His aim seemed to be to talk it through with someone to feel heard and consequently feel better about the situation. Typically, the information was exchanged between people who may not have worked together but had good relationships—spouses, colleagues in other organizations, friends, family members, and so on. Rarely did this translate into information that informed the actions inside the organization.

Empathy

Managers also engaged in corridor feedback as a means to relate to others in the organization. They wanted to let others who may have similar problems know that they were not alone. For example, a new office manager was engaged in a budget struggle with the higher management. A more experienced colleague told her that she too was involved in a similar struggle and went on to say that most managers face the same challenge. The emphasis seemed to be on communicating that she was not alone and that the more experienced manager could relate to her problems. This information was often exchanged between co-workers of the same level and rarely translated into information that formally informed future actions in the organization.

Exploration

If a manager was not sure about personal thoughts or feelings, the manager might choose to explore them with someone outside the feedback arena. Through this conversation, the manager might consolidate an opinion, gather the opinions of others, or brainstorm new ideas and suggestions. A manager's exploration usually occurred with a boss or a close colleague. Interestingly, only sometimes did exploration seem to translate into information that formally informed future organizational actions. A manager might choose to raise new ideas in the next official arena or not.

Coalition Building

Managers often talked behind the scenes to create or renew connections, get people onto their side, convince people to see issues or people from their perspective, or see whether people agree or disagree with an idea. Some coalition building was done in healthy ways in which people felt honored. On other occasions, behind-the-scene coalition building fueled adversarial relationship among people, felt threatening, and promoted gossip and unchecked generalizations about people. This process sometimes led to information that influenced future organizational actions.

Circumvention

Managers frequently worked around the meeting bureaucracy in order to get things done. For example, a manager might talk privately with another and decide to go ahead with a new policy in order to sidestep the lengthy meeting process. Or a worker might go over the head of his or her boss to get support about a particular idea. In this kind of behind-the-scenes talk, people seemed skeptical that any actions could be generated from the current public mechanisms of processing in place. Therefore, in order to advance the idea or action, corridor talk was necessary. It was extremely rare that this mechanism offered any formal feedback to the system.

Lack of Safety

If managers did not feel safe or comfortable in a meeting, then they were not able to offer helpful and constructive feedback. Managers in meetings sometimes felt that they did not have the freedom or authority to critique or offer suggestions. They felt that if they did so, it might disrupt the group, give the impression of attacking people or put themselves at risk. Giving feedback outside of the arena seemed safer. When they gave feedback directly to the principal actor, then it translated into useful information.

CORRIDOR TALK REFLECTION SHEET

	Never	Some-times	Fairly Often	Always
How often do you engage in corridor talk?				

Think of a recent experience of corridor talk. What motivated you to engage in it? Check all that apply.

	No	Somewhat	Yes
Catharsis			
Empathy			
Exploration			
Coalition Building			
Circumvention			
Lack of Safety			
Lack of Value			

	Never	Sometimes	Often
How often do your colleagues engage in corridor talk?			

What do you think primarily motivates your colleagues to engage in corridor talk? Check all that apply.

	No	Somewhat	Yes
Catharsis			
Empathy			
Exploration			
Coalition Building			
Circumvention			
Lack of Safety			
Lack of Value			

To curb unhealthy corridor talk, list some strategies you could do to:

Make people feel safer in meetings:

Make people feel valued in their work:

Reduce bureaucratic obstacles to action:

Invite people to publicly discuss ideas or issues that they may have processed outside of meetings:

Better solicit and manage public disagreements and conflicts:

Lack of Value

Some managers seemed to share confidential information on how they really felt with a colleague outside of meetings because they wanted to feel valued or important in the eyes of that colleague. In the case of Ismael and Maria Jimena, they might choose to talk with Clare because they want to feel valued by Clare. The researchers speculated that this motivation might also be tied to a workers sense of loss of control. If workers felt that they were losing control and responsibility, then they might choose to engage in corridor talk as a means to reassert an image of control in the eyes of their colleagues. Corridor talk could allow them to save face and revive a perception in others that they were still important and in the know. Rarely did this information ever translate into formal feedback about the actions in the organization.

In order to help managers think critically about how they managed corridor talk in their personal practice and in their offices, the researchers devised the reflection sheet presented on the following page. It invites managers to consider the quality of their corridor talk and guard against the destructive tendencies. Although the tool asks them to check boxes that represent rough qualitative and frequency categories, these categories are not of primary importance. The conversation that happens about the reflection tool is the focus.

Lessons in Crafting Smarter Cultures

For five months in the third year of the project, investigators worked closely with three managers and their office personnel to build smarter office cultures. Communication was an important focus of the research. The investigators looked for changes toward a smarter culture of communication, drawing on their own observations and gathering quantitative and qualitative pre- and post-assessments from the office workers and their clients within La Tadeo. Many important lessons emerged about how smart tools impacted the culture of the university offices.

Tools such as these cultivated a higher level of *trust, honesty,* and *respect* in the offices (italics represent key words and phrases used in interviews and written assessments). Evidence for this appeared in the development of the workers' language and interactions over the five months. For example, some participants created more space in meetings for discussions of *personal emotions, worries,* and put themselves in *vulnerable positions.* Such honest reflection and surfacing of personal feelings gave rise to a few complex situations in some offices. For example, some participants shared buried feelings of jealousy and inadequacy in their offices. Such trust led to many delicate and complicated areas of inquiry that required long-term explorations by the group. Through this process, the researchers felt the participants grew to *have more awareness and support of each other, see other facets of their co-workers, have deeper personal relationships,* and *feel more valued and respected as a human being* in the organization.

During the five months, the researchers also observed growth in how the offices *examined* and *resolved problems.* The researchers observed a stronger sense of *group reflection, collective examination,* and *shared problem solving* in the offices. For example, initially, one office depended almost entirely on the boss for problem analysis and solution. The boss simply instructed the workers about how to act. After six weeks, the personnel processed problems more collaboratively, gleaning perspectives and solutions from almost all the office members. To support more collaboration and communication, all offices adopted a policy of *weekly meetings* (as suggested by the researchers). In these meetings, participants developed skills around *consensus building, listening, conflict resolution, feedback, how to craft personal roles,* and how to develop *shared office missions*. As these meetings evolved, the researchers noted *better management of defensive behavior, increased interaction on difficulties and solutions, more focused engagement,* and *more concrete and clear communication* among the participants.

The survey data drawn from 25 participants in three offices seemed to suggest a similar trend. During the five months, participants rated themselves on a scale between 1-5 based how well them saw themselves engaging in particular practices. Over the five months, there were marked increases in the participants' perceptions of how well the offices *gathered internal feedback, suggestions and new ideas to better its performance* (group averages rose from 3.04 to 3.40), how well individuals *drew on different perspectives and experiences to build ideas and solutions* (group averages rose from 2.81 to 3.23) and how well the offices *collectively reflected, evaluated progress, and made decisions in order to better its performance* (group averages rose from 2.91 to 3.28).

However, the researchers also observed some obstacles in developing smarter cultures of communication. Chapter 1 summarizes many of the challenges that leaders and organizations face when crafting cultures that support learning. What follows are two specific barriers that continually surfaced and threatened the development of smarter cultures of communication in La Tadeo:

Time and Pressure

The constant stream of emergencies, crises and tight deadlines reduced the time available for managers to try out new communication strategies reflectively. Indeed, particularly in emergency situations, not every conversation needs to be or can be generative. However, when the office environment became overwhelming, managers often reverted to their old habits and entrenched strategies. However, sometimes they found creative ways to reflect and try out new actions—for instance, keeping journals or car pooling to reflect with colleagues. Finding sufficient time and freedom from pressure to support the learning of new ways of thinking and acting always was a challenge.

Clear Modeling and Reinforcement

The researchers observed that tools and practices of smart communication did not slide into place easily. Having a few workshops was not enough. Even when managers were convinced that a tool was terrific, adopting new patterns of communication proved complicated. In order for smart tools and practices to survive and thrive, they needed clear modeling by culture makers—the leaders, managers and workers who held the respect of the group and affected the patterns of communication. When people began to adopt the tools, managers needed to reinforce their use, giving thanks and praise to the users. When people dropped a tool, the manager needed to step in and reorganize the interaction. Unsurprisingly, some managers took on this role more readily than others.

Such lessons clearly point to the role of leadership in sculpting smart communication habits specifically, and cultures of understanding in general. In the next chapter we will continue with this theme and examine how leadership can better foster learning in organizational cultures.

Reflection

In what ways do you find the culture of communication around you "smart?" In what ways not so smart?

What are the main challenges you face in creating or contributing to a smart culture of communication around you?

How might you best begin to infuse these ideas (Generative Conversation, Ladder of Feedback, Healthy Corridor Talk) into your practice? What would be good first steps?

Action

When you next find yourself giving feedback, try to implement the Ladder of Feedback: first clarify, then signal positive features, then share possible concerns and suggestions.

Adopt the Ladder as a standard feature of meetings where a lot of feedback is given.

When a colleague comes to you with a problem, try to play out the principles of Generative Conversations (and not degenerative!).

Before and after meetings, rate your performance using the Generative Conversations evaluation. Introduce the tool to a group and do this collectively.

Convene a small group of colleagues to talk about Healthy Corridor Talk. Encourage each other to model its use. Reflect on what difficulties arise.

5. Leadership for Learning

Jesus and Margarita

Jesus and Margarita were veteran administrators at the university with very different leadership styles. Jesus' office workers regarded him as the expert and ran all decisions and information past him. When problems arose, Jesus simply instructed his workers what to do and checked in with them to ensure that they did it. When his office was small, Jesus had few problems with this style. However, as his office and his responsibilities grew along with the organization, he felt overwhelmed. He simply did not have time to track everything. When he could not make room in his schedule to monitor all the workings in his office he felt that he was losing control. When workers took matters into their own hands to deal with emergencies, he got angry and frustrated with their mistakes. His office gradually became paralyzed by his need to have information about and power over all matters.

Margarita, whose office was down the hallway, had a different leadership style. Early in her management career, Margarita, like Jesus, was very hands-on. However, as her office expanded, she learned to let go of her need to micro-manage, and began teaching and trusting others. As with Jesus, daily organizational crises often interrupted Margarita's work. However, in such moments, Margarita interacted quite differently with her workers. When they came to her to report emergencies, they arrived with possible solutions in mind. Margarita gave few direct orders. Instead, she posed questions, inquiring about background information, asking for opinions, and encouraging her workers to consider alternative solutions. Afterwards, Margarita scheduled post-crisis reflection meetings with her office personnel during which everyone involved could learn from the handling of the issue. In general, Margarita empowered each person to make a range of decisions and expected them to be accountable for the results. She did not goad or hover over her workers. Instead, she saw her role as facilitative, fostering their work by cultivating their ideas. As Margarita told the researchers, adopting this new style was not easy nor did it happen overnight. It was a slow process of experimenting and adjusting her practice.

Previous chapters examined how ideals, tools, and actions function as culture makers, at their best developing cultures of organizational understanding in action. Jesus' and Margarita's cases illustrate another central element in fostering organizational understanding: how certain leadership styles support individual and collective learning. As noted in chapter 1, leaders too are culture makers. Their actions play an integral role in providing models and constructing supportive environments where workers can safely act and thoughtfully reflect in order to close the idea-action gap. This chapter explores what leadership for learning looks like. It shows how leaders at La Tadeo shaped cultures of learning through three concrete tools that project investigators developed with managers at the university. In conclusion, the chapter highlights how this type of leadership influenced La Tadeo, as well as outlines traps that leaders must avoid in order to bridge the idea-action gap.

Leading Across the Gap

Whether a particular manager is more like Jesus, more like Margarita, or something in between, the challenges of organizational life come with the package. There is always an issue of balancing the direct use of one's authority with delegation of authority. When delegating, there are questions of how tolerant to be of others' different styles and occasional mistakes. There is always a tension between getting things done expeditiously and making room for people to learn by doing. There are always crises, where time may not allow practices that in calmer moments serve the organization better. There is always the risk of operating almost continuously in crisis mode.

Although such challenges are intrinsic to organizational life, different styles of leadership can exacerbate them or reduce them. Jesus' style of leadership tended to exacerbate them. His reluctance to delegate and to make room for people to learn left him taking on too much and left him subordinates ill-equipped to take on more, as well as frightened to do so, lest they displease him. More crises were a natural consequence, pushing the office into a continuous survival mode. In contrast, Margarita's leadership style, by striking a different balance, allowed people to grow in response to the expanding complexity of the office's responsibilities.

How then did the management scene at La Tadeo appear? Inevitably it was a mix. Hearteningly, some university managers crafted leadership practices that fostered learning. Managers like Margarita, spanning different levels of the organizational hierarchy, seemed committed to developing people's understanding in their work. We came to call this leadership style *leadership for learning.* Such leadership helped the people working in an office to cross the idea-action gap, translating ideals and strategies into action effectively day in and day out. The researchers noted that the leaders who developed such a style had four main elements in common. These elements receive further attention in the upcoming tools section as well:

Encouraging Exploration

Leaders like Margarita encouraged their colleagues and workers to explore and experiment with their practical actions. Whether in response to an emergency or a routine situation, such managers urged their colleagues to consider new ways to act. Leaders for learning also modeled this with their workers by sharing their own questions and explorations. They backed this up by facilitating reflection and offering informative and non-threatening sources of feedback. Such experiences allowed people to build new repertoires of beliefs and actions about work.

Engendering Action

Leaders for learning publicly gave their colleagues and workers good reason and motivation to try out actions. Though many in the university tended to avoid action, substituting talk, leaders like Margarita made thoughtful action paramount. They offered safe environments in which to act, provided social support, gave rewards, fostered ideals, and sustained a coherent and consistent philosophy and framework that got people moving.

Scaffolding Thinking

Leaders for learning also supported the cognitive demands of the process. Margarita and others helped people think about what they were doing before, during, and after they did it. These leaders were careful observers who helped others catch the right moments for action and reflection in the midst of a busy day. Often, leaders used questions to provide such cognitive support. This scaffolding of thinking allowed workers to build up a repertoire of thoughtful moves.

Managing the Dark Side

Finally, leaders like Margarita displayed a cunning craft of managing elements that threatened progress. They minimized negative forces by, for instance, mediating conflicts, encouraging people not to expect miracles overnight but rather incremental progress, and encouraging skeptics to raise their opinions in constructive ways. They also monitored their own natural defensiveness and insecurities, factors that could, in the fast pace of organizational life, erupt and threaten the culture of learning they were trying to create.

With its focus on learning and on closing the idea-action gap throughout the organization, leadership for learning contrasts somewhat with many views of leadership. Writers on organizational leadership such as Max DePree and John Gardner suggest that effective leadership involves humanistic characteristics such as clarity of vision, human empathy, moral integrity, courage, energy, and curiosity. Certainly, the authors of this book agree that these are important traits up to a point. However, we would want them to lead to learning, closing the idea-action gap and deepening understanding in action throughout an organization. A leader could have energy, but, badly exhibited, it could threaten the idea-action gap. Another leader could have a clear vision, but not create safe places for colleagues to think and act. With such points in mind, we find that leadership for learning focuses more on encouraging exploration, engendering action, scaffolding thinking and managing the dark side.

How can leaders cultivate leadership for learning? As emphasized in chapter 1, tools can foster change. This chapter presents three tools concerned with leadership for learning: *Leadership through Questions, The Bermuda Triangle*, and *Trust*. Similar to the tools presented in previous chapters, these tools had different histories of development and saw different degrees of use within La Tadeo.

Leadership through Questions

Eduardo was a manager in charge of the physical maintenance of the university. One morning, one of his crew chiefs interrupted a meeting with a problem. Only a few painters had appeared for a job. To top it off, they did not bring the appropriate equipment. Cursing, Eduardo excused himself from the meeting, went back to his office, and searched for the phone number of the paint contractor. When at last he found it, he handed it to the crew chief and told him exactly how to handle the contractor in order to fix the problem.

Across the hall, Susana went to her boss with some questions on a purchasing order. After she gave her boss a quick update on the purchases, her boss told her to solve it herself. "You figure it out," her boss said. "Do what you have to solve it." Susana returned to her desk, re-examined the order, and picked up the telephone to see whether another office had the information she needed to understand and fix the problem.

Javier, a manager in the computer systems department, got a visit from a co-worker about a system crash. Javier suspected he knew exactly why the system crashed. However, he held back his response. He instead asked his co-worker questions and gathered information about the crash. In fact, it turned out that Javier's initial intuition about what caused the problem was wrong. He asked his colleague how they might avoid a crash in the future. After a five-minute conversation, the worker left, eager to try the handful of solutions that he had generated.

Leadership is a tricky business. The styles of Eduardo, Susana's boss and Javier illustrate of the ways university leaders interacted with their colleagues. Some leaders readily imparted knowledge and solutions. Other leaders tended to leave people alone. Others tended to engage in conversations with workers. Some leaders acted one way in some situations and another way in others. Clearly, different situations, pressures, and personalities contributed to the variety of leadership styles that the researchers observed.

This not withstanding, some approaches seemed to foster learning and close the idea-action gap better than others. During the fall of the project's second year, investigators closely observed four managers in practice and noted their different leadership styles. The four managers were generally considered effective managers throughout the university. The researchers developed the Leadership through Questions tool to reflect their techniques and, over a period of a few weeks, checked the tool with these managers and refined it. Then the researchers shared the tool with the larger group of managers through workshops and the weekly meetings. Other managers practiced using the tool and a few implemented the tool in their action projects. The tool began by introducing three styles of leadership:

Leading through Answers

Many times when problematic situations arose, leaders had an immediate solution. Because they had little time or because they viewed the problem as trivial, they simply gave the solution and orders on how to handle it. This was leadership through answers. Leaders who exclusively use this type of leadership viewed themselves as the primary and best source for solutions. Often this strategy was the most efficient in the short term. However, in the long term it could backfire. It risked undermining the emotional investment of the workers as well as depriving them of opportunities to learn. In the opening illustration, Eduardo demonstrated this leadership style.

Leading through Abandonment

In other situations, leaders did not give solutions, guidance or support at all. A leader might instead say, "Look, you solve it. That's your responsibility," or "Just try and figure it out." The researchers called this tough-love style of leadership leading through abandonment. At its best, this style was very efficient: The worker solved the problem. However, many times workers did not and often they committed strings of errors. In any event, the message to the worker was clear: "Don't come to me with your problems. You figure them out, and if you screw it up, you're in trouble." In the opening examples, Susana's boss illustrated this style of leadership.

Leading through Questions

Some leaders, like Javier, did not simply give answers or abandon the worker. Instead, they constructed a conversation in which the worker explored and created solutions to the issue at hand. The leader assisted, but more as a facilitator. The investigative team called this leadership style *leading through questions.* The leader posed genuine questions designed to gather information. The leader allowed workers to think about the problem at hand, generate their own solutions, analyze the options and construct a plan of action.

In the Friday meetings, managers reflected on their practice using these three types of leadership. They asked themselves: Do I tend to use a particular style? When do I? Managers also examined cases and dialogues, and critiqued them using the three types of leadership. In small groups, the managers made suggestions about how a leader could better redirect a *leading through answers* approach to a more genuine *leading through questions* approach. The managers soon discovered that Leadership through Questions was not just about asking any old questions. Successful display of this leadership style hinged on the type of questions asked. For example, "Don't you think that is a dumb idea?" or "Why don't you use my solution?" are certainly questions, but ones that undermine the learning process. With such examples in mind, managers found it helpful to contrast two types of questions:

Conducting Questions versus Constructive Questions

The two questions above are common examples of conducting questions. They are rhetorical. When leaders put such questions to someone, it was clear that they wanted not so much a considered response as agreement and action. The question was simply a form of communicating that demand. When first introduced to leadership through answers, many managers found themselves using conducting questions, in effect reverting to a surreptitious form of leadership through answers.

In contrast, constructive questions allowed people to create their own ideas or solutions. Sometimes these ideas and solutions needed to be negotiated with the leader, but the questions were sincere invitations for people to build their own thoughts, based on their own analysis. "So what options do you see? What has worked in the past? Which strategy do you think will work better?" were all fine examples of constructing questions.

A Guide for Leadership through Questions

In order to help university leaders further refine their use of questions, the investigators developed a guide. Managers practiced using this guide in small groups in the Encuentros. The guide contained the main principles and particular types of questions they could ask, outlining the basic steps in Leadership through Questions.

Creating a comfortable environment: Those leaders who displayed a commitment to learning often made moves to create a comfortable space, feeling and tone. They invited people to sit, asked them if they wanted tea or coffee, made conversation to create ease, made physical contact, smiled, and so on. Such leaders seemed be very aware of how their body language and physical space communicated a message of interest in people and their ideas. Such leaders often came out from behind their

Leadership through Questions

Goals

- To guide people to discover "insights"; their own ideas and solutions.
- To guide people through questions of thinking and analysis.
- To create constructive (not aggressive) and exploratory interactions.

Key Moves

Create a Comfortable Environment
Before engaging in the conversation, leaders create a situation that is safe and comfortable. They are careful of their body language and how they have arranged your furniture. The environment communicates interest in the person and their ideas.

Gather Information
Before giving reactions, leaders take the time to collect important data, facts, circumstances which surround the context. Examples: "Tell me more about...," "Could you explain...," "What happened...," "What led to this...," etc.

Probe for Suggestions
Leaders engage others in exploring their own suggestions, ideas or solutions to the issue at hand. Examples: "What options do you see?" "What are your ideas?" "What suggestions do you have?" etc.

Invite Analysis
Leaders ask others to evaluate suggestions by weighing pros/cons, or ponder the consequences of their suggestions. Examples: "What are the pros/cons of your suggestions?" "Which suggestion do you think would work best? Why?" "What would happen if we took this suggestion?" etc.

Synthesize and Check
Leaders create a shared conclusion/recommendation and check with people for agreement and understanding. Examples: "Based on your ideas, I see this option... what do you think?" "I like your suggestion, let's do it, okay?" "Based on what you are saying, perhaps we can do this... do you agree?" etc.

desks, wrote ideas down in notes, and nodded to signal attention and interest.

Information gathering. Before offering ideas or a position, such leaders gathered information about the situation with queries such as, "Tell me more about..." "Could you explain ..." "What happened..." and "What led to this..."

Probing for suggestions. Leaders skilled with Leadership through Questions invited workers to share their ideas to solve the problem at hand. For example, leaders would say, "What options do you see?" "What are your ideas?" "What suggestions do you have?" Investigators noted that such moves led to employees feeling more trusted, respected and valued in the office. Also, engaging workers in devising their own solutions seemed to raise their investment and produced better follow-through.

Inviting analysis. Leaders often asked their co-workers to evaluate suggestions by pondering consequences and weighing pros and cons. Leaders said things like, "What are the pros and cons of your suggestions?" "Which suggestion do you think would work best? Why?" and "What would happen if we took this suggestion?"

Synthesizing and checking. Finally, the investigators noted that leaders adept at leading through questions often summarized a conclusion from the interaction and checked it with people for agreement and understanding. For example a leader might say, "Summarizing what you said, we should probably do X. Do I have that right?"

Leading through questions was one path that managers took towards leadership for learning. In conclusion, it's worth connecting the idea of leading through questions with the four characteristics of leadership for learning mentioned earlier: encouraging exploration, engendering action, scaffolding thinking, and managing the dark side. The tool of Leadership through Questions encouraged leaders and the led to explore together in an open spirit how they understood problematic situations and actions to deal with them. Leading through questions engendered action by motivating and scaffolding others to come up with their own plans, in which they would have an investment. Leading through questions also placed a high priority on scaffolding the thinking of others. Leaders asked workers to analyze causes, suggest possible solutions, and pro and con them. And finally, like all good leadership for learning practices, this tool managed the organizational dark side, disarming potentially explosive situations and making people feel safe and valued.

The Bermuda Triangle

Elena, the leader of a human resource work group, was trying to improve the training courses for secretaries. In a weekly meeting, she discovered that Ciro did not do what he promised: administer a training needs evaluation to a small group of secretaries. Ciro said that he simply did not have the time. "I didn't know that I had to get written permission from each secretary's boss for them to fill out the survey. I didn't have time to do all that on top of everything else this week," he explained.

Elena was peeved with Ciro's lack of follow through. Moreover, last week others in the group had failed to do what they said they would. Faced with a pending deadline and her own promises to her boss, Elena found herself at a crossroads: Should she give the task to someone else? Should she confront Ciro in the meeting and teach the group a lesson? Should she get different people to work in this group? Should she scrap the timetable for the new training program altogether? Elena took a deep breath and contemplated her options.

Elena's situation will be familiar to any manager. To indulge in a nautical metaphor, all too often, on the high seas of management at La Tadeo, the water was rough. Between charting the course, mapping the progress to the horizon, keeping morale high, and reading the weather signs for approaching storms, some leaders expressed a feeling of being lost at sea. Nevertheless, many leaders seemed to navigate well. How? The researchers working with these leaders found a clue. The skilled pilots avoided becoming overwhelmed in a *Bermuda Triangle* that sank many crafts.

The *Bermuda Triangle* is an image the researchers adopted to represent three different directions managers often felt pulled in during stormy situations: product, process, and person. In Elena's case, she felt that perhaps the people simply were not getting on with the tasks and producing the products they should. Perhaps she should press for action. At the same time, she wondered about problems of process: Perhaps Ciro and the others became bogged down in paperwork and bureaucratic rules and lost momentum. A revised process might be the solution. Also, she wondered about the people themselves. Perhaps they were not personally involved with or motivated by their work. What could she do to secure their commitment? Whatever she chose, not only the solution to the immediate problem but also learning was at stake. An emphasis on product could help people to develop persistence and systematicity. An emphasis on process could dismantle old and cumbersome processes and help her staff to learn new ones. An emphasis on person could cultivate more commitment, fulfillment, and personal growth. The question was, which was right for the occasion?

Interestingly, this trio of product, process, and person corresponded to the three bottom lines identified in chapter 2—productive, operational, and humanistic criteria for success. Not uncommonly, managers found themselves caught in a three-way magnetic pull among them, a Bermuda Triangle indeed. Successful leaders seemed to consider the three and find a course of action that chose an appropriate corner or struck an artful balance. Abstracting from their experience, the researchers formulated the tool of the Bermuda Triangle to help others become better pilots in dangerous waters. Let us consider the three corners of the triangle in more detail.

Product: Effective Results

Leaders within the organization often judged the effectiveness of a group by looking to products, outcomes, or results. Such attention is, of course, an essential element. However, researchers on group behavior, such as J. Richard Hackman, point out that leaders often measure success and diagnose difficulties

Emotional
Investment

Efficient
Processes

Effective
Results/Products

by products alone. In La Tadeo, leaders who myopically cared only about final results often jeopardized other factors important for a thriving organization, for instance, the quality of human relationships. Elena felt tempted to insist that her staff move forward briskly. That might indeed be the right solution, but she recognized that the problems might lie elsewhere.

Process: Efficient Procedures

The second corner of the triangle concerns procedures that are quick, frugal, and smooth. Often thing went wrong at La Tadeo not because people were not trying, but because procedures were cumbersome. Many times leaders needed to examine and refine the ways in which they and their co-workers worked in order to use time, money and other resources better. Even when leaders saw offices producing good results, if the costs were high in time and resources, they might step in to reorganize the process. Elena recognized that such a factor might figure in her situation.

Person: Emotional Investment

Astute leaders also recognized the importance of working closely with people, so that they felt valued, respected, and personally invested, and believed in the journey. Elena wondered whether Ciro and others felt sufficient commitment. To be sure, she could threaten them, but that certainly would not generate commitment, just superficial obedience. Without her cultivating emotional investment, her efforts to correct the goals and method of work would seem autocratic and would provoke cynicism and disengagement in the office.

Which corner of the triangle to choose, or what balance to strike? The Bermuda Triangle offers no one answer, because good answers vary from situation to situation. However, it did provide a reflective tool that helped managers to recognize the dilemmas they faced more clearly and choose a path more wisely. The researchers introduced this tool in the weekly Friday meetings with managers. Although it did not receive the emphasis given to leading through questions, several managers began to employ it. They soon became more aware of moments of learning in their offices. Elena, for example, quickly evaluated the pressures of product, process and person. She decided that, in her particular situation, a lack of emotional investment might be standing in the way. This was the immediate problem and also the learning opportunity for people. She took the time in the meeting to figure out how to involve people personally in moving the work ahead.

Trust

Gloria, the leader of one of the financial offices, asked Martin and Alvaro to meet with her about some billing problems. Gloria had considered inviting Susana, but Susana and Martin had had many problems working together. They had even refused to work together on certain projects. Gloria could not afford to get side-tracked in figuring out this billing problem. Though Martin and Alvaro had never worked together, Gloria had supreme confidence in Martin since Martin had always come through for her in the past.

Alvaro arrived forty minutes late to find an impatient Gloria and Martin. Being a little late was not so unusual at La Tadeo, but 40 minutes for an important gathering was a bit much. "Sorry I'm behind," sighed Alvaro. "The traffic this morning was terrible." Gloria remembered hearing that Alvaro was a bit disorganized. His tardiness confirmed this, she thought.

"I know the traffic is a pain," Gloria said somewhat sourly. "But look, Alvaro, we have to allow for these things. Anyhow, let's get moving now." Gloria had begun to wonder if she could trust Alvaro to work with her and Martin to solve this problem. The trio was off to a bad start.

Gloria's experience was not atypical. The project researchers noted that many organizational tensions grew because of problems of trust. To be sure, there were many reasons for strained relationships—competitiveness, jealously, abrasiveness, and divergent working styles. However, the investigative team speculated that, in addition to other factors, deep controversies usually involved failures of trust. It was not just a matter of getting along. Martin did not *trust* Susana, and Gloria was beginning not to *trust* Alvaro.

Accordingly, the researchers developed a tool around trust and the factors that breed distrust, often unnecessarily. In workshops, managers learned about mistrust, how it is formed, how it can escalate and how it could be contained in relationships.

How are trust and mistrust bred? Observing situations like the one sketched above, project investigators concluded that people form *trust models* of one another—mental models of how much each can be trusted. People construct these mental models from the other person's role, hearsay about the person, and first impressions. As people gain further experience, they update their trust models through direct evidence.

The problem is, trust models can easily deteriorate into mistrust through several mechanisms, with considerable risk of self-fulfilling prophecy. The factors that send trust models spinning off-track are the same sorts of factors that trouble many other kinds of mental models. They tend to involve over-interpreting others' symbolic conduct. Researchers working with university leaders named the following as typical factors:

Unreasonable Expectations

Leaders sometimes expected paragons of ability and commitment, building an unreasonably glowing trust model. They "angelized" someone. Then, when the person did not entirely live up to those ideal expectations, often the trust model flipped over to a sense of profound disappointment and betrayal, "demonizing" the person instead of angelizing, which is also unreasonable. For example, a project manager felt betrayed when a colleague unexpectedly left a project with relatively little notice, although enough notice to satisfy institutional requirements. Later he concluded that his trust model had been unreasonably idealistic. Although the colleague was committed to the project, an exceptional opportunity presented itself. It would not have been sensible for him to pass up the opportunity.

Unclear Shared Expectations

It was easy for people working together to have different tacit conceptions about one another's performance. When violations occurred, trust plummeted. In their well-known 1982 book, *The One Minute Manager*, Kenneth Blanchard and Spencer Johnson underscore how commonly managers place unexpected expectations on their subordinates. Accordingly, the practice of one-minute management starts with a process of one-minute goal setting, yielding a statement of goals in less than a page that can be read in less than a minute. Although this may be heavy-handed for many situations, trust is more likely to be reasonable when expectations are shared and clarified in one way or another.

The Fundamental Attribution Error

This social psychology concept concerns how people explain their own and others' actions. People tend to account for their own actions by situational factors but others' actions by character or personality. Why was Alvaro late for the meeting? Alvaro might say quite honestly, "I spilled coffee at breakfast and had to clean it up, and then on top of that the traffic was terrible." Someone else like Gloria might say, "Alvaro's a late kind of guy." Both accounts could have some truth in them. However, leaders needed to be careful of generating sweeping personality attributions since they tend to lead to overly negative or positive trust models, demonizing or angelizing. Underscoring the risks, sweeping attributions to others' characters thrived in what chapter 4 referred to as the managers' corridor talk.

Overgeneralization

People readily generalize from one dimension of trust or distrust to another. Gloria was worried because

> **Five Factors that Influence Trust Models**
> - Unreasonable Expectations
> - Unclear Shared Expectations
> - Fundamental Attribution Errors
> - Overgeneralization
> - Selective Information Processing

Alvaro's lateness might mean that he could not be relied upon in other ways. Perhaps. However, when we think about our friends and colleagues, it is easy to find people who are entirely trustworthy in one way but not so trustworthy in another. One might, for example, trust a friend to baby sit one's children but not trust the friend to water one's plants reliably while one is away. Likewise, even if chronically late, Alvaro might be very trustworthy in many other respects. A good trust model for Alvaro would be differentiated, not sweeping, specifying the areas where Alvaro could be most trusted rather than over-generalizing across all areas.

Selective Processing of Information

The researchers noticed that some leaders treated certain people as though they could do no wrong, while treating a few other people as though they could do no right. Like mental models of all sorts, trust models, once formed, generated selective processing of information that tended to confirm them. Once a leader had reached a conclusion, the mixed and messy evidence of everyday relationships was likely to strengthen it. Once an angel, always an angel. Once a demon, always a demon. It might take a virtual avalanche of contrary evidence to change a leader's trust model about someone.

The moral of all this could be put in a single phrase: *trust models were not to be trusted.* Like other mental models, they often needed to be surfaced and scrutinized. The angry reaction managers felt when trust seemed to have been violated might be appropriate, but could easily be an overreaction. Likewise, the serene confidence they felt in another might have been overconfidence.

Although trusting too little and too much were both problems, the researchers concluded that trusting too little was more of a problem. It's best to trust a little too much (not a lot too much!) than a little too little. This is

Guidelines in Cultivating Healthy Trust Models

- *Don't demonize.* If your distrust in someone seems profound and sweeping, don't trust your trust model. Consider bringing your trust up a notch or making it more differentiated.

- *Don't angelize.* If your trust in someone seems idealistic, don't trust your trust model. Consider bringing it down a notch. Are your expectations idealistic or reasonable? You may be setting yourself up for a flip into profound distrust, the tragedy of trust.

- *Be Objective.* If you feel that events keep confirming your deep trust or distrust, don't trust your trust model. Stand back and take an objective look. Are you processing evidence selectively? Are you creating the situation you see by the Pygmalion effect (which could be good) or reverse Pygmalion effect (not good)?

- *Clarify.* A person committed to reflective trust clarifies expectations. If expectations are vague, get them out on the table and negotiate conflicts in a positive win-win spirit.

- *Pygmalionize.* Trust a little more than you think you objectively should. Get Pygmalion on your side.

because of something psychologists call the Pygmalion effect. People's belief in another's positive attributes, and consequent nuances in their behavior toward that person—what chapter 2 called symbolic conduct—tend to bring out and strengthen those very attributes. If Gloria trusts Alvaro, Alvaro will read this in her behavior and try to live up to that trust. Likewise, there is a reverse Pygmalion effect: Belief in another's shortcomings may well exacerbate them. If Gloria does not trust Alvaro to try hard, Alvaro is likely to detect this and, feeling alienated, not try very hard. Thus, trust breeds trust and mistrust breeds mistrust.

Leadership for learning inevitably involved refined perceptions of who could be trusted to do what. It's almost a cliché to say that good leadership inspires trust—both trust in the leader and trustworthiness on the part of those that are led. The good leader even displays just a little too much trust, because it is always good to have the Pygmalion effect on your side.

Lessons about Leadership for Learning

Certainly leadership for learning is a challenging endeavor, one often difficult to exercise within organizations. At La Tadeo, the managers faced many leadership challenges, and, to be sure, many personal and organizational obstacles persisted throughout the project. Nevertheless, the tools described above and others like them produced some interesting results.

In the spring of the project's third year, the researchers worked closely with three university offices. The researchers observed the leaders of these offices in action and supported the leaders in reorganizing their practices toward learning. The researchers noted three interesting themes in the offices that helped to close the idea-action gap:

Increased Personal Meaning

Using pre and post surveys and observation notes, the project researchers found that office workers felt that their work had more personal meaning. Likert scale surveys, using a scale of one to five, of 35 managers from three offices showed that group averages of personal meaning at work rose from 2.82 to 3.54. Leaders in these offices were co-constructing visions and goals with the workers, asking them to reflect on their work, engaging them exploration, and supporting them in action.

Increased Collaborative Problem Solving

From the same pre and post surveys, project investigators noted significant increases in how the personnel felt about their collaboration skills. The workers felt that the leader was allowing them to build better ideas together, drawing on a variety of resources and perspectives to solve problems (group averages rose from 2.81 to 3.23). They also felt that the leader was opening more spaces for reflection on and evaluation of the office performance (group averages rose from 2.91 to 3.28) In general, the workers felt this empowered them to make decisions about improving their actions and the actions of the office.

Avoiding the Learning Traps

As a final theme, the researchers also found that successful leaders were acutely aware of and avoided four pernicious traps that often threatened to thwart their leadership for learning: *answers, power, pressure,* and *distrust.*

Answers. Successful leaders avoided the expectation that they had to know all the information and have every solution in advance. If a leader feels she must know everything, then not knowing the answers fosters defensiveness, which might take the form of authoritarian gestures or angry outbursts. Avoiding the answer trap meant managing such feelings by taking time-outs and like methods. Succumbing to the answer trap threatened the learning of others and interfered with their ability to bridge their own idea-action gaps.

Power. Successful leaders also abandoned the need to have power or control over every situation. They recognized that many of their colleagues viewed power as the way to gain the respect of their workers. However, they disagreed. They believed that it was not necessary to make all the decisions autocratically. They were not worried about appearing to be weak. They were not afraid of changing their minds or encountering proof of a mistaken decision. They saw that the power trap, like the answer trap, limited the learning of themselves and their employees. It enlarged the idea-action gap by making people feel threatened and unable to explore innovations.

Pressure. Too often, pressures motivated managers to become action addicts—they thrived on a fast pace and the adrenaline of the pressure. But the best leaders in our study viewed this as myopic. It did not support the learning of others, since it focused on the leader as the main actor. Of course, overcoming the pressure trap was an inherent challenge in La Tadeo, as in other organizational settings. Crises inevitably arose, last minute demands occurred, and quick decisions at times had to be taken. But the best leaders managed such moments with honesty and clarity with their workers.

Distrust. "If I want something done right I'll do it myself" was the final trap that leadership for learning avoided. Often, leaders had developed elaborate beliefs about whether various co-workers could be trusted to perform or to learn and develop. These beliefs, once set in the mind of a manager, were difficult to move. Information about and experiences with a co-worker were filtered through this pre-established mental model. Not trusting others clearly limited the ways in which they learned and grew, and how they closed their own idea-action gaps. The best leaders carefully scrutinized their own models of trust.

To summarize, leadership for learning points organizations toward leadership practices that more clearly and publicly support individual and group learning. It also involves moves that help to close the idea-action gap. This chapter has introduced tools that support such a style of leadership. Leadership for learning involves managing the *Bermuda Triangle* of tensions between product, process, and person to exploit potential moments of learning in the everyday flow of work. Leadership for learning favors *leading through questions* with constructive rather than conductive questions over *leading through answers* and *leading through abandonment*. Leadership for learning involves an understanding of how distrust can grow like a disease to interfere with work in general and learning in particular, and how trust can be cultivated. Finally, leadership for learning involves skirting four traps: the traps of feeling that one must know all the *answers,* have all the *power,* respond immediately to *pressure,* and broadly *distrust* those who do not live up to the highest expectations.

Leaders certainly are in positions to foster learning and in general promote understanding in action. However, what is the larger picture? When an institution as a whole makes a commitment to such an approach, how can the leaders and participants organize such an initiatives? What structures and roles serve the purpose? The next chapter deals with these questions.

Reflection

What is leadership for learning? How would you define it?

What strategies do you currently take in your organization to foster learning when you find yourself in a leadership role?

This is a challenging one: Try to identify times when you behave in one or another of the three leadership styles identified here—leading through answers, leading through abandonment, and leading through questions. (And there are certainly times when the first two may be appropriate.)

Think back to a moment of crisis that you managed well. Recall one that you managed poorly. Map your actions using the Bermuda Triangle.

Notice your trust models. Are you demonizing? Angelizing? Being objective? Are you trusting too little or too much?

Action

When you next find yourself interacting with some colleagues over a crisis, try to enact a Leadership through Questions style. Jot down some reflections and note what questions you used that seemed to work well.

The next time you find yourself trying to make an awkward decision that involves people factors, try out the Bermuda Triangle to see whether it clarifies the dilemma. Reflect afterwards on how it worked out.

Think of someone you think might respond if you showed a little more trust, maybe even more than seems warranted right now. Try it as an experiment.

Convene a small group of colleagues to talk about leadership styles. Consider what moves you all make that support or inhibit learning in individuals, groups, and the organization.

6. The Architecture of Growth

A Day in the Life

The highpoint of the Encuentro that morning was Maria's story. She had been talking over ideas for an action project with her staff and had reached the conclusion that she wanted to work on creating a database of the contracts her office had to deal with.

For many people, such work would be simple. Her problem was that nobody in her office really knew much about technology and they only had one computer to share among five workers. This made things difficult. At the Encuentro, she described her dream to her colleagues and they started asking her questions. Who can help you? How much data do you have? Do you have access to the contracts?

All the questions led her to identify the mysteries she had to solve. She needed to have access to files, she needed to get at least one more computer, and she probably needed access to the Systems department for consultation. The Vice-Rector for Management was attending the Encuentro. After hearing the story, she felt persuaded by Maria's cause. She said she should speak with the lawyers about file access and bring Maria's proposal to the Systems committee. Maria's friend Pablo also let her know that he was attending an Understanding in Action group that included several people skilled with databases. He invited her to the next meeting.

Before Maria knew it, she found herself in the middle of an action project with more people helping her than she had ever expected. Hard work lay ahead. She responded to the interest the other members of the Encuentro had shown. She became responsible for attending the meetings with the lawyers, getting the consultant, and letting him know about her interests. Her project had begun in earnest.

The Architecture of an Initiative

As the foregoing story illustrates, any project that works at all, works day by day. It works through the gatherings that happen, the conversations that occur, and the individuals and groups that accept key responsibilities. It works not just because people have new ideas, but also because behaviors change to express and sustain a different culture, one more collaborative and more oriented toward learning.

The previous chapters have foregrounded particular tools and patterns of activities. In this chapter, it's worth standing back to consider the structure and style of the entire initiative, the configurations that have kept Understanding for Organizations in motion. It's also worth examining some of the challenges of sustaining participation, their nature, and approaches to dealing with them. Accordingly, the sections to come review the support structure critical to the initiative: key groups and their roles, the regular patterns of activity, and general principles of building a culture of learning, such as cultivating internal expertise and fostering modeling by top managers. We then consider how marginal participation and stirring up suppressed issues created special challenges.

As throughout this book, certain sources inform the thinking. At the very general level of analysis advanced in this chapter, a scheme offered by Lee Bolman and Terrence Deal in their 1997 *Reframing Organizations* proves illuminating. Bolman and Deal introduce four organizational frames (in our terms, one might say lenses) for viewing an organization: the structural, human resource, political, and symbolic frames. More than anything else, Understanding for Organizations was aimed at *human resource* development, fostering individual growth and more effective collaboration to get the work of the organization done in a responsible and creative way. However, to advance this cause, the project established certain *structures* within La Tadeo. This in turn required *political* support. Fostering a culture of learning within the organization also depended on the *symbolic* side of organizational conduct, corresponding to the symbolic conduct lens discussed in chapter 2. Thus, all four frames figured in the Understanding for Organizations initiative.

With its emphasis on a culture of learning, Understanding for Organizations also resonated with Edgar Schein's discussions of culture in organizations. Schein holds that organizational cultures reflect sustained tacit beliefs about basic values, human relations, and overall purposes. In keeping with this, the present initiative led people to examine and sometimes challenge beliefs embedded in practices at La Tadeo, promoting somewhat different beliefs. At the same time, the initiative developed a strong emphasis on action. Just as new beliefs might lead to new actions, so might new patterns of action foster new beliefs. We sought to play it both ways.

With these preliminary remarks in place, let us consider the structures and political supports, the symbolic gestures and associated beliefs and values that moved Understanding for Organizations forward. In keeping with the emphasis on review, the pages to come offer an assembly of lists, an effort to articulate concisely and systematically the elements in the mix of Understanding for Organizations. The architectural emphasis might suggest that individuals who are not highly placed in an organization will find little here that is actionable for them. However, the chapter concludes with a section, "But I'm Only One Person..." that brings forward a range of opportunities for action.

Key Groups and Roles

Any big or small initiative depends on individuals and groups in different roles, carrying out different functions. This was certainly true at La Tadeo for Understanding for Organizations. The top administration helped to organize and implement a structure that sustained the work day to day. The key roles in this structure are summarized in the table *Key Groups and Roles* and discussed one by one below.

Political Leadership and Support

The principal players here were the Rector of the University, Evaristo Obregon, and Vice-Rector for Management and Finances Fanny Mestre. These two championed the effort as well as arranged for financial support, space, and related matters. They attended some of the larger and smaller meetings held with the participating managers. They were seen as symbolic figures, showing a major interest in the initiative, without which it undoubtedly would have faltered.

Project Management Team

An interdisciplinary and intercultural four-person team managed the initiative on-site, including three members of La Tadeo's community—Dora Bonnet, Cecilia Miani and Juan Sastoque—along with Project Zero researcher, Daniel Wilson, who lived in Bogotá during most of period of project development. This Project Management Team organized the processes for building the framework now in use, conducted meetings, counseled participants, and generally advanced the project on a daily basis. The team met regularly on Tuesdays and Thursdays and brought together ideas, experiences and concerns from the week before. They planned the Direct Participants Group activities, and documented the process. They wrote newsletters for the participants in which they highlighted the advances in the achievements reached. They maintain telephone and email contact with the External Guidance Team and also carried out research studies to evaluate and improve the initiative.

Key Groups and Roles

Political leadership and support, from the top administration.

The Project Management Team, people who guided and facilitated the day-to-day work of the project.

The External Guidance Team, people who visited from Harvard regularly, probed the literature, and played a key role in developing the framework and research plan.

The Direct Participants, the managers who directly participated in meetings and led action projects and other initiatives that involved many others.

The Internal Experts, several direct participants who worked closely with the Project Management Team and helped with coaching others.

The External Guidance Team

Three members of Harvard Project Zero, David Perkins, Chris Unger, and Veronica Boix-Mansilla, searched the literature widely and developed concepts, organized the writing of reports, and visited La Tadeo for a week four times a year, joining in a variety of activities and presentations with the top administration and the various groups participating in the project. They worked closely with the Project Management Team in co-constructing the ideas, the frameworks, practical tools, and research designs. They located the new ideas within the state of the art, provided a sound theoretical basis, and generally advised the Project Management Team. Together with the team, they were the architects of the framework.

The Direct Participants

These managers and staff members administered various areas of the university and had a special interest in seeing things change. Initially, there were about 25. By the writing of this book, the initiative had directly touched about 70 managers and involved about 110 of their colleagues and corresponding subordinates in action projects. They were invited to take part in order to develop commitment and accomplish improvements. They were there because they wanted to be there. They were direct participants in that they played roles that involved considerable contact with the Project Management Team and, when in town, the External Guidance Team. Many other people in the administration of the university played a role in the project through their offices—typically offices led by direct participants. But the direct participants were the culture makers.

Members of this group had multiple roles. They formed smaller groups for the construction of ideas related to the lenses discussed in chapter 2. They planned and executed action projects to try out different ideas in practice. They became observers of their own actions at the same time that members of the research team observed and worked with them toward reducing the idea-action gap. They met every Friday to advance particular initiatives, and they attended monthly general meetings and Encuentros where the discussions tested the emerging theories from an intellectual perspective. They were the participants that carried the innovation forward with ideas and action, day by day, in the offices of La Tadeo where it counted.

The Internal Experts Group

This group of especially interested and committed administrators at La Tadeo evolved during the second year of the project. These managers — Ramón Carrillo, Jaime Melo, Guillermo Forero and Luis Eduardo Mantilla — were also Direct Participants. The Project Management Team and External Guidance Team felt that internal experts would aid the initiative in several ways. By gaining greater sophistication about the initiative, they would provide it with more long-term presence and stability within the university. They could also aid the initiative day by day, trying out new ideas and working with other participants. Indeed, members of the group served as coaches for the project managers and facilitators in meetings and Encuentros. They tested new strategies, gave feedback, and often co-constructed strategies with other team members. Because they were also functioning as managers at La Tadeo, they promoted and supported the new culture when members of the Project Management Team could not be present. They used the ideas in action and also served as examples for others.

In summary, these five groups, working together, made Understanding for Organizations a going enterprise. The groups played complementary roles. To remove any one would have been to impair the effort greatly.

The Activities

The five groups could be seen as the characters listed at the beginning of a script, the *dramatis personae*. But what was the play and how did it advance a culture of learning? The Project Management Team and the External Guidance Team organized several regular activities that simultaneously helped to build a culture of learning and investigated and improved the process along the way. A summary appears in the table *Key Activities* table and a fuller account of each follows.

Friday Meetings

Friday meetings became a ritual. The upper management of the university officially committed two hours on Fridays week in and week out for the participating managers to reflect on and advance the work. Managers could, and often did, find other moments in their schedule. But those two hours were reliably there. The Friday times were used for various purposes: organized reflection sessions, workshops, Encuentros, retreats outside the university, and meetings of the Lens Groups and Action Project Groups to advance the ideas and give support to the people taking them to action. All the

Key Activities Summary

Friday Meetings, time officially set aside for general or more focused meetings among the administrators to advance the project.

Lens Group Meetings during the first year and a half of the project.

Action Projects pursuing individual and small group objectives from the second year on.

Understanding In Action Groups, where 4-6 managers interacted over time on separate or unified projects in their respective offices.

Mentor Meetings, to coach participants in the initiative.

Encuentros, minicourses to introduce people to the initiative.

Office Interventions, action projects in individual offices beginning with an office assessment.

groups mentioned in the previous section participated in various combinations in these sessions. More often than not, the meetings associated with the activities listed below occurred during the precious Friday time slot.

Lens Group Meetings

As mentioned in chapter 2, the project had different phases. The 25 managers who made up the initial Direct Participants divided into three groups corresponding to the three organizational lenses of symbolic conduct, generative life, and care. These groups of six to twelve managers met most Fridays for two hours to explore their chosen lens and its applications to individual and organizational practices. They organized their work around observations of their own actions and experiences from the perspective of their lens. They gave and received feedback, and produced tools, strategies and other documents to share with others in the project and the organization. A member of the Project Management Team facilitated each of these groups.

The Lens Groups were the principal working structure aside from whole-project meetings for almost two years. The Lens Group discussions and activities yielded many insights about administrative life at La Tadeo and helped the participants to become culture makers. In later years, these participants met through the Encuentros and the Understanding in Action Groups. This structural shift occurred in part because one goal of the project was to explore different structures. It happened largely because, as the conversations developed richly over time, participants declared that they wanted to understand all the lenses equally.

Action Projects

Personal, group or organizational action projects (see chapter 3) became a focus beginning about half way through the first year. The Friday time and other moments arranged by the participants provided for planning, informing, and giving feedback to one another. In order to develop more community commitment, action projects had a public face. All Direct Participants had access to what each member was doing and could find occasions to offer support to others. In general, the meetings around action projects were occasions for learning to value the organized and meaningful work of others rather than to criticize it negatively. They were moments for advancing the integration of human, operational, and productive considerations—the three gauges of development introduced in chapter 2.

Understanding In Action Groups

Finally, the project evolved toward small learning teams, the members of which explored their understanding in action. Groups of four to six managers worked together on a weekly basis on cultivating practices of understanding in action in themselves and others. Frequently, managers invited other managers into their offices to observe the action in a meeting, a presentation, or other event. Beforehand, the manager briefed the Understanding in Action Group on the context, what issues the manager was working on, and perhaps areas where specific feedback would be welcome. After the hour of observation, the group reconvened to share perspectives, offer feedback, and contribute suggestions. Managers rotated in making their offices available for observation. Though clearly the managers being observed learned a tremendous amount, the observers also gleaned ideas and strategies from watching their co-workers in action.

These groups varied their practices according to their needs and interest. Some groups decided to design a collective action project made up of smaller ones. On Fridays they discussed their progress and difficulties with their common agenda. Others pursued the same idea in their separate offices and pooled experiences at their meetings. Still others simply met to inform one another about the progress of distinct action projects and seek counsel.

Mentor Meetings

These were one-on-one meetings between a manager and a member of the Project Management Team or one of the Internal Experts. They were opportunities to get feedback and advice on how to improve individual or office action projects. Frequently, office hours were held, during which managers could set up appointments. Typically these meetings lasted about an hour. During them, the mentors listened and offered counsel concerning not only professional matters but also the personal dimension of life and interactions at La Tadeo.

Encuentros

Encuentro in Spanish means gathering. Several times a year, the Project Management Team and the Internal Experts offered Encuentros to recruit new participants and share the project ideas with them. These gatherings were in some ways like mini-courses. Typically they involved weekly sessions of two-hours, lasting from 10 to 12 weeks. New participants heard about the ideas, tried them out in their own work settings, shared their organizational experiences, and read and discussed relevant literature. At the end of the Encuentro, these participants had the options of joining the project and working with cadres of managers on these ideas, or not becoming involved with the project.

Office Interventions

One of the last initiatives offered by the Project Management Team involved working with the head of an office and all its staff, using feedback about the office from multiple sources as a starting point. Employing a systematic set of questions, people within the office evaluated both their own beliefs and behavior and those prevalent in the group. Clients of the office offered their impressions using a similar set of questions. All reports were anonymous. A member of the Project Management Team assisted the director of the office in carrying out this process. Based on the data received, the director and staff organized action projects and other initiatives to improve the office. Sometimes this involved restructuring how a particular role functioned, or recasting individuals in different roles.

Principles and Practices for Building a Culture

As outlined above, several groups and several patterns of activity made up the structure of Understanding for Organizations. However, such a project requires more than columns and beams, floors and ceilings. As essential as structures were, just as important was a set of core practices and broad principles to help sustain a culture of learning in an organizational setting. All of these aimed not just at promoting new ideas but fostering new patterns of behavior—much the greater challenge. The practices and values became realized to varying extents, but they informed the effort throughout. They are listed in the table *Principles and Practices for Building a Culture,* with a paragraph on each to follow.

Clear Focus

In Understanding for Organizations, creating and maintaining clear coherent strategies was both important and challenging. It was important because participants wanted to and needed to know the aims and scope of a strategy and how they might act effectively. It was challenging because, as was often said during the project, we were "building the boat as we sailed it." Ideas, vocabulary, and techniques evolved over time through practical use, evaluation, and modification. Because of this changing strategic landscape, what became most important was not strong adherence to the minutiae of particular strategies but overarching ideas such as the commitment to understanding in action.

Learning in Different Moments

Different kinds of learning occur in different moments and on different time scales. One continuing aim was to respect this reality and indeed take advantage of it. The moments of learning could be mapped along three dimensions: long term versus short term, planned versus spontaneous, and in-the-moment versus out-of-the-moment. Encuentros were calculatedly long term, planned, and out-of-the moment. Action projects emphasized the long term and moved back and forth between out-of-the-moment reflection and in-the-moment action. Some action projects and some strategies introduced in the Encuentros sought to inform spontaneous action and to foster learning in-the-moment—for instance, strategies for conducting meetings or giving feedback.

Internal Expertise

Many change initiatives fail to develop expertise internal to the organization. When the team guiding the change reduces its role, people within the organization lack the know-how to carry on. The project adopted practices through which people inside the organization could learn in general, receive mentoring, and eventually mentor others in understanding in action. A constant criterion for the development of strategies asked to what degree a strategy fostered the development of internal expertise. These efforts benefited the Direct Participants and especially the Internal Experts.

Rich Social Interactions

The project focused on generating moments when participants could interact and reflect on three levels: individually, in small groups, and as a community. For good results, it seemed essential to touch all three of these levels. Adhering to a core tenet of social constructivists, this emphasis led the leaders of the project to design approaches that would be flexible, allowing participants a range of ways to build ideas and process knowledge collaboratively. As with other principles central to the project, the aim was to develop a culture of growth and improvement based on action, reflection, and communication, and not simply to attach a new methodology to an existing culture that remained untouched.

Modeling by Top Managers

It is common knowledge that without support from the leadership of an organization, such a project would have tremendous difficulty in succeeding. Indeed, as already mentioned, Understanding for Organizations enjoyed the public support of the top figures, including the Rector and the Vice-Rector for Management and Finances, both of whom initiated the project. Verbal support is certainly important. Moreover, when the leaders, key managers, or other power and culture brokers in the organization modeled the ideas in action, this always increased momentum. In contrast, when such figures sometimes displayed conduct that contradicted the tenets of the initiative, the participants in the project felt discouraged, cynical, and confused. Therefore, we adopted strategies that gave top management the chance to lead, model, and cultivate understanding for action on the organizational stage. For instance, leaders were encouraged to show their action project to their subordinates and to receive critique, as well as critique action projects of others, in the spirit of equity.

Balancing Humanistic, Operational, and Productive Concerns

Chapter 2 introduced three values that informed this initiative throughout. Understanding for Organizations tried to keep this triarchy in balance when measuring the project's impact: humanistic (concerned with people's beliefs, needs, comfort, energy, and well-being generally), operational (concerned with effective and efficient structures and processes), and productive (concerned with producing high quality, and where appropriate creative, results and products). Many change initiatives emphasize just the second or third of these. The leaders of this initiative believed that a healthier culture of learning results when all three received balanced attention.

Principles and Practices for Building a Culture

- *Clear focus,* despite changes in particular strategies.

- *Learning in different moments,* on various time scales.

- *Internal expertise* cultivated.

- *Rich social interactions,* fostering reflections individually, in small groups, and as a community.

- *Modeling* by top managers.

- *Humanistic, operational, and productive concerns* in balance.

- *Empowerment of participants* to pursue worthwhile innovations.

- *Trust and respect,* not only in words but in actions.

Empowerment

The project aimed to cultivate a sense of agency and create a responsive setting in which people could act effectively. The long-term momentum of the practices introduced would depend upon this. The various techniques were designed to cultivate a sense of accountability and responsibility, encouraging people to monitor their actions and creating safe ways through which they could make their work more public and receive and give feedback and support.

Designing strategies and fostering activities that promoted a sense of trust and respect among the managers was also important to creating a culture of learning. People were encouraged to show trust and respect not only through words but actions such as sharing ideas, giving constructive feedback, revealing fears, etc. In the same spirit, the initiative sought to discourage behaviors that generated adversarial relationships, cynicism, jealousy, and defensive reactions. Considerable effort was made to promote healthy patterns of communication, often with good results.

Fostering Wide Participation

The foregoing ideas paint an ideal, even an idealistic, picture. Inevitably, the reality did not always live up to the aspirations. As with most projects, a few participants were highly enthusiastic and energetic, some were skeptical and reluctant, and most fell in the middle, doing worthwhile work within the scope of their immediate activities. As the project developed, the challenge became not only to promote action projects, Encuentros, and the like, but also to foster wide participation. This included encouraging marginal participants to get more involved, and to protect the project from perceptions that participation was weak and from polarization between participants and skeptics.

Involving Token Participants More

As mentioned, about every three months the External Guidance Team visited the university, attended general and smaller meetings, helped to design and offer workshops, and addressed the participants. Top management usually joined these activities as well. During these high-profile periods, it was common to see better attendance and higher energy. Some participants who might need particular support for a project, or who sought simply to be on the scene, appeared, only to vanish for weeks afterward.

Other participants who sustained a regular presence did so in a marginal way, showing up at meetings, tucking in a word now and then, and occasionally applauding the effort. Although certainly more would be desired, such contributions were valuable as far as they went.

One particularly vexing aspect of token participation occurred around action projects. Some participants would undertake small-scale action projects that never seem to get very far. Such participants might talk about an impressive project, but the reality amounted to much less. Sometimes this seemed to be artful hypocrisy, sometimes a kind of self-deception, and sometimes a genuinely frustrated scrabble to cope with the many expectations imposed from different directions.

After discovering this pattern, the Project Management Team adopted a general strategy to cope with it: a more intimate and finer-grained process of assessment. One-on-one conversations with participants created a setting of dialog where peripheral participation tended to show up for what it was. Such settings were not meant to be threatening. If some participants were not able to invest themselves as deeply or energetically as others, that was accepted. A generous-hearted but clear vision of who was really doing what seemed to help some to become more active.

Reframing Token Participation

Although the token participants were in a minority, the mere presence of that minority occasionally generated a political problem. Others noticed the irregular pattern of contribution and felt discouraged. They registered such circumstances as signs that the initiative was faltering.

Besides encouraging fuller participation, the Project Management Team sought to deal with this problem by reframing people's perception of token participation. The Project Management Team and External Guidance Team asked people to think about other initiatives they had experienced. Was token participation to be found there as well? Of course. Were there also particularly enthusiastic and effective participants? Yes, there were. Indeed, typically initiatives of change generate what might be called a bell-shaped curve of participation, with many contributing moderately and usefully while a few fall at the extremes. This way of looking at token participation helped members of the administrative community at La Tadeo to see token participation as part of a normal pattern rather than as a cause for alarm.

Avoiding Polarization

In many change initiatives, the leaders make a different response to token participation: Single out those genuinely interested and treat them as a special group, planning to involve the others later, after establishing momentum. Richard Elmore, in an article on the conditions of change, cautions about the risks of such a tactic. To focus resources on the champions and leave the rest alone tends to create two cultures, the "ins" and the "outs," breeding resentment and rivalry. The bell-shaped curve of participation polarizes into two bells, one representing the protagonists of the initiative, the other the antagonists. Such a situation tends to destroy the initiative in the long run.

To avoid polarization, Understanding for Organizations adopted calculated measures to keep everyone as involved as they felt ready for, without undue pressure but with a welcoming face. Peripheral participation was better than no participation. People who did not often show up remained on mailing lists and received notification of meetings. When they did appear, others welcomed them into the conversations as smoothly as possible. Remembering that people have different rhythms, different styles of learning, and different moments in which human beings get interested and find meaning has been essential to the initiative. Such a strategy has trade-offs. One cost may be that people feel less pressure from above to declare themselves clearly in or out of the effort; however it was well worth this cost in La Tadeo in order to avoid polarizing the group.

Handling Controversies Positively

Processes of organizational inquiry have a paradoxical side effect: Although intended to make things better, they often aggravate concerns that previously stayed submerged. We sometimes called this *stirring the swamp.*

In the very first year of the project, when the three lens groups of Care, Symbolic Conduct, and the Generative Life were in full swing, such challenges began to emerge. Participants looking through those lenses started to see things they had not seen before. Rivalries and animosities, as well as mismatches between philosophy and practice that previously had been overlooked or only idly noted, sometimes became the center of heated discussions.

Such events have both a positive and a negative aspect. On the positive side, it is a sign of growth that concerns can come to the surface. On the negative side, the concerns may threaten the status quo so much that they generate a backlash against the project. The Project Management Team did its best to accentuate the positive and diminish the negative. Along the way, the members of the team learned and deployed a number of tactics, used in various combinations as the occasion suggested.

- *Acknowledging hotspots.* When a sensitive matter emerged and the conversation started to escalate, it was often important to make people explicitly aware of that. "Look at what's happening! We've touched a nerve! People feel strongly about this. Let's recognize that."

- *No premature burials.* Attempting to bury or dismiss sensitive matters when they come up would have been a mistake, suggesting a fundamental dishonesty in the conduct of the project.
- *Soon but not now.* When a sensitive matter erupted unexpectedly, the best time to deal with it thoroughly was not necessarily *now*. Often it was better to acknowledge the matter as a serious concern and make a specific plan for attending to it in the near term.
- *Venting on the side.* Often people needed to vent their concerns. They needed to speak out frankly, in muddled and even crude ways, before standing back and taking a more detached and analytical look at a problem. But extended venting in large meetings can easily hurt others deeply. It was better to create occasions for venting on the side—for example private one-on-one conversations.
- *Unpacking and framing.* Often examining a difficult issue in a group setting went better if the facilitator brought some kind of preliminary analysis of the issue to frame the discussion. This could be based on prior informal conversations with some of the people involved.
- *Honoring positives.* Most issues have more than one side. It was helpful to ensure that the positive side got more than perfunctory floor time, not to mask the negatives but to acknowledge the complexity and honor what was good. To do otherwise was to encourage a bleak and unforgiving atmosphere.

From Sweeping Solutions to Smart Solutions

Tactics such as those listed above helped to create a more positive climate. Even so, the question remained how to resolve the concerns that surfaced. Admittedly, reaching a full solution usually was considerably more difficult than calming things down. That said, the facilitators made an effort to guide the participants away from sweeping solutions and toward smart solutions.

For many sensitive points, the first ideas to come to mind had a sweeping character—*never, always, forbidden, completely free to, condemned, applauded, "in," "out."* The challenge was to get beyond these sweeping ideas to a more nuanced approach. For example, in one group a discussion flared up about a group member responsible for a key office. Other members said that this office did not produce important monthly figures on time. People tried everything they could to get the office chief to accept the blame. However, with the theme of symbolic conduct in mind, the conversation gradually evolved beyond this scapegoat approach. Other participants began examining the conduct of their own offices. Eventually, they discovered that the problems did not emanate from the office originally blamed but from a chain of delays in the offices feeding information to that one.

In general, smart solutions are more nuanced than sweeping ones. They recognize different needs and circumstances and complex causes. They make adjustments. Also, often smart solutions are more than just compromises—X gets some of what X wants, Y gets some of what Y wants. They have the quality of a synthesis. Thus, they take time, effort, analysis, and invention to work out. They accommodate feelings deeply and seriously, but they are not simple translations of people's feelings into some sweeping action. Over time, the Project Management Team tried to steer difficult conversations toward smart solutions—sometimes fruitlessly but sometimes with success.

"But I'm Just One Person..."

As promised, this chapter has emphasized the architecture of Understanding for Organizations—the groups and roles, the patterns of activity, the larger-scale principles, and the moves made to encourage participation. A natural response to such a collection of elements is, "But I'm just one person..." To be sure, the emphasis has been on the large scale. That acknowledged, it is important to ask what all this says to just one person. The answer, unsurprisingly, depends on what sort of a position that one person has within the organization in question.

Really One Person

Suppose that you really are just one person among many, not an authority figure, not even a member of a closely integrated working group. How does any of this apply? It's worth considering the question in terms of the three categories of groups/roles, activities, and general principles/practices:

- The sorts of groups and roles discussed in this chapter do not make much sense for you. They are all larger-scale structures.
- By and large, the activities also do not make much sense. They all involve groups. However, you can conduct individual action projects. Indeed, many administrators at La Tadeo did exactly that, focusing on their own specific needs and opportunities, although within the context of small groups that provided conversational support and feedback.
- Even as one person, you can adopt some of the general principles and practices. You can strive to learn in different moments, with different rhythms. In your own work, you can seek to balance humanistic, operational, and productive concerns. You can behave toward others with trust and respect.

In addition, it's worth emphasizing that many of the tools discussed in chapters 2–5 apply very well to individual action. You can look at events around you through lenses such as symbolic conduct, care, or the generative life, you can apply good practices of communication, and so on. The architectural emphasis of this chapter should not mask the many resources in earlier chapters that suit the individual.

One of a Group

In any case, chances are you do not meet the profile of "really one person." More likely, you are a member of one or more close working groups, coordinating your action with others in the group. In such circumstances, more opportunities open up. It's worth visiting the same set of categories again.

- The groups and roles discussed earlier in the chapter all had a special purpose—supporting Understanding for Organizations. Simply being in a group with some other purpose does not create opportunities there.
- However, many of the activities could be advanced within your group, if you bring them to the table and champion them successfully. In addition to collective action projects, you might promote setting aside a regular time—analogous to the Friday meetings—to pursue group needs and opportunities. You and your colleagues might undertake action projects that begin with a systematic assessment of the work of your group and continue from there with a program of innovation, as with the Office Interventions discussed earlier.
- As to general principles and practices for building a culture, the group context allows for most of these to come into play. You and your colleagues as a group can try to sustain a clear focus and to foster learning in different moments. You can strive for rich social interactions, maintain a balance among humanistic, operational and productive concerns, and commit yourselves to patterns of interaction that maintain trust and respect.

Of course, along with the group context will come questions of marginal participation. If the group undertakes an initiative at all, some are likely to be energetic enthusiasts, some in the middle, and some token contributors. The strategies discussed earlier for dealing with this apply to the small group context just as well as to a large-scale initiative.

Leader of a Group

You may be more than a member of a group. You may be a leader of a team, of the workers in an office, of the personnel of a small store. It may be just one group in a much larger organization, but even so, within that group you have great influence as a culture maker. To visit the categories again...

- Looking at the category of groups and roles, you are in a position to offer political leadership and support to initiatives within the group. You are also in a position to foster the development of internal experts who take particular responsibility for moving innovations forward.
- In terms of activities, you have the power to allocate time for meetings, promote action projects, design office interventions, and, if you choose, function as a mentor to individuals.
- In terms of general principles and practices for building a culture of learning, virtually all apply. In particular, an important addition from simply being a member of a group is your position to empower people in particular roles by delegating authority.

Of course, your position of power also generates a risk. Leadership positions are generally a little lonely, and they can become more so! If you impose the ideas discussed in this book, or other ideas like them, without sensitivity to existing patterns and expectations, you may generate resentment and a backlash. As with leadership at any level, projecting a vision that inspires commitment is generally more effective than simply imposing an agenda that people do not understand or appreciate.

Top-Down and Bottom-Up

If your position in an organization is relatively high—not just the leader of a group but of a department or division—you are in an even better position to act. You could, if you wanted and given approval from your superordinates, establish an initiative very much like Understanding for Organizations, with some appropriate variation of its activities and substructures, using your leadership skills to inspire attention and mobilize action.

However, we would like to caution against an entirely top-down view of the ideas threaded throughout this book. We would discourage the notion that only high-level leaders can advance such a cause effectively. Even as "really one person" or "one of a group," you always have opportunities for action. Moreover, sometimes cultural changes grow and thrive in a bottom-up rather than a top-down manner. Your actions as an individual, as a member of a group, or as leader of a small group may affect not only yourself and those who work with you, but those who see what is happening, become curious about it, gain inspiration from it, and pick up and promulgate its spirit and practice.

It would be misleading to suggest that such things happen commonly or easily, but they do happen. Above all, the authors of this book want to encourage people to act in their circumstances as best they can. As emphasized in chapter 1, the real challenge for any agenda of change is the idea-action gap, the difficult passage from visions, goals, and strategies to making something happen in the world. Therefore, we encourage you to act wisely and proactively with the principles laid out here, or—because we recognize that there are many paths toward better individual and organizational life—with others that express a similar commitment.

Reflection

Which of the groups mentioned in this chapter would you like to lead, and why?

What structures does your organization currently have to support change? Imagine you are a CEO who has to present an innovation to the board of directors. Envision the innovation and design the basic support structure you would need, capitalizing on existing structures.

Every time you go to a meeting, think of why you go. Is it as a token participant, a steady participant, or a proactive participant? Why?

How would you handle token participation and controversies surfaced by a change initiative?

Action

Design and move forward an innovation, perhaps just a small scale one, thinking about the key groups and patterns of activities that would sustain it.

Create and implement a strategy to help you keep in balance the humane, operational, and productive dimensions of your work.

Before acting, think about what kind of culture you will be promoting through your actions. Try to act in a way that fosters a culture of learning.

Identify a controversy within your organization that you are in a position to mediate (this may mean that you yourself do not have a strong public position). Use the ideas suggested in this chapter, or others, to try to steer the controversy toward a smart rather than a sweeping resolution.

7. Toward a Culture of Learning

The Waters of Culture

This book tells the story of how a new framework and set of tools for supporting organizational learning was developed. Within this tale lies a subtle and nuanced plot: how to foster a shift in culture, one that signals a new way of perceiving, thinking, valuing, and acting in an organization as a whole. Organizational theorists like Edgar Schein posit that the culture of an organization largely reflects the tacit values and beliefs that regulate the actions and interactions of the people in an organization. These tacit values and beliefs, along with the patterns of behavior they yield, are almost invisible to the participants in the organization. As fish, who live in water all the time know nothing about water for lack of contrast, so people who participate in an organization often have little awareness of its distinctive cultural characteristics. We simply live in the cultural waters, which go unquestioned and, usually, continue unchanged.

Yet change appears to be possible. In this chapter, the authors take a close look at cultural change by way of the four culture makers initially presented in chapter 1—ideals, leaders, tools, and actions. We review these leverage points for change through three stories of shifts in attitude and behavior at La Tadeo.

Felipe's Office

Things had not been going well in the Office of the General Secretary, which took responsibility for logistics: student enrollment, grade follow-up on students, the time tables of courses, and the distribution of space for classes and other duties related to teachers' services at La Tadeo. Staff members found themselves working overtime, getting anxious about the growing backload of requests, and becoming depressed and annoyed at the frustration and anger that often came with those requests. Moreover, everyone in the office seemed to be trying to survive by themselves, on their own island. When interaction occurred, it was often unpleasant, with people blaming each other for work not done.

Felipe, the head of this department, was a member of the Generative Life Group, which emphasized reflecting about well-being and personal fulfillment. For the first time in the twenty years Felipe had worked at La Tadeo, he began to feel that he could show himself without masks. He found himself able to share his thoughts with his colleagues at a personal level. He felt supported and encouraged to act differently.

Felipe cared for the members of his staff, and did not like the growing uneasiness and tension in the Office of the General Secretary. He decided that something had to be done. Pleasantly surprised at the growing feeling of camaraderie in the group as he began to open up, Felipe decided to share the problem solving with them. He asked his staff members whether they would be willing to stay a little after work every Wednesday to discuss what was happening in the office and how things might go better. In compensation, people could come in late on some morning, decide to leave early, or take a break in the afternoon to handle personal tasks during work.

How to manage the meetings was a question. Recalling ideas from the Generative Life Group, a project researcher and Felipe decided that they should start each meeting asking, "What is working well here?" Continuing from there, "What is not going so well?" And finally, "What can we do about it?" The purpose of the meetings was anything but blame and punishment. The staff members pooled their thoughts to figure out how they wanted their office to run. The staff became proactive, feeling empowered to be creative and close the idea-action gap.

Over time, people devised new strategies for engaging in their work. They found ways of supporting each other, including how to attend to particularly difficult workloads and accompanying anxieties. A greater sense of community and belonging developed. Impressed by the solutions that emerged from working and thinking together, people began to care more for each other.

In summary, Felipe's participation in the Generative Life Group helped him to become a culture maker for a different kind of culture in the Office of the General Secretary. Felipe became acutely aware of his and others' feelings while at work, and of the prospects for change. Felipe adopted new actions himself, which broadcast new ideals, and he introduced a formal structure with a simple inquiry tool for exploring how the office functioned—the Wednesday meetings with the three key questions. All this shifted others' perceptions and behavior in his office, fostering a new way of attending to work through attending to one another and one another's needs.

Claudia's Department

During this same period, Claudia, one of two heads of the Continuing Education Department, participated in the Symbolic Conduct Group. Recall that this group emphasized how words and actions often conveyed positive and negative attitudes beyond the specific context—attitudes about trust, expectations, risk, and other matters. The members of the Symbolic Conduct Group came to understand that the culture of La Tadeo was in part created through the kinds of memos sent, the style of interactions in the corridors, the words and gestures of colleagues, and many other factors that were part of the texture of everyday life. With the help of the facilitator, the group had begun to critique the culture with insight, seeing the need for reflection and mindfulness toward building a new culture. They also emphasized the importance of balancing the humane, operational, and productive aspects of the office—the three platforms or bottom lines introduced in chapter 2.

The Continuing Education Department was a product of the unplanned growth of the University. It had a mixed mission that sometimes proved awkward. On the one hand, the department organized courses offered to people not enrolled at the university as regular students, as programs of continuing education generally do. In this respect, the department was responsible to the central administration. On the other hand, a chain of circumstances led to the Continuing Education Department taking responsibility for organizing courses for the regular academic program in which students completed projects that were prerequisites for graduation. In this respect, the department was responsible to the Academic Vice-Rector. In general, different philosophies about teaching and the design of such courses generated considerable confusion.

The managerial life of the office displayed a growing disorder. The former boss had quit, leaving behind innumerable problems and administrative confusion. In response, the central administration had decided to temporarily place two people in charge, rather than appointing a single chief of the office. Claudia was one. In principle, the two managers were to address different fields of action—Claudia handling administrative issues while Pedro looked to academic matters. But things did not work out this way in practice. Both Claudia and Pedro felt that they had something to say about both areas. Moreover, they had quite different ideas about what types of courses should be offered, how curricula should be developed, how to evaluate courses, and how to distribute managerial duties, handle the income, and contract with teachers. Both felt empowered to give orders to the staff members, creating disorder and duplication of functions. Each staff member worked in his or her corner, feeling isolated and confused. A patina of harmony and respect concealed a conflict of interest, with two contrasting managerial approaches. Gossip was the main source of information. Sides were taken. The atmosphere was charged.

Inspired by her involvement in the Symbolic Conduct Group to take an interest in tackling the problems, Claudia began to discuss the current situation with her office workers. She decided to develop an action project that might allow her to improve the situation, involving the staff in the process. She defined her own dream for the office, with everyone functioning as a harmonious team. She identified the principal mysteries, such as how to approach her colleagues without polarizing them. She planned the actions to be taken first, such as listening to every member of the staff.

Finally she launched her action project, using the members of the Symbolic Conduct Group to provide feedback. Applying some of the tools discussed in chapters 3 and 4, Claudia began to understand more deeply the very real problems of her area. She used some of the leadership tools discussed in chapter 5, asking questions and giving enough space for her staff to propose initiatives. She also began to develop a respectful conversation with Pedro, the other interim boss.

With some difficulty, redirecting her process each time the evidence revealed problems, Claudia managed to establish better patterns of communication within the micro-culture of the Continuing Education Department. In addition, she called on the research team to guide an office intervention. This began with weekly meetings in which everyone participated. All the staff members in turn described their functions. This exercise in itself brought to light many incoherencies, duplication of tasks, and different points of view on the same issues, as well as misunderstandings of the office's mission and place within the University.

Rethinking the office was a huge task, patiently undertaken by all members of the staff. The whole group began to walk towards a common dream that replaced the managerial and ideological chaos. With time, the group redesigned the office procedures. Communication improved enormously. Weekly meetings created a forum for reporting successful or unsuccessful actions and exploring issues. The Ladder of Feedback, with its pattern of clarification, valuing and suggesting, became the norm.

In summary, Claudia initiated a change in culture. She led by example. She took actions and encouraged others' actions that fostered a new mindset. Tools for more constructive forms of communication and leadership came into play. Ideals were articulated and pursued. The four Culture Makers took hold.

Luis's Office

Meanwhile, members of the Care Group had begun discussing the importance of looking after the assets of the University—not only material, but human. This focus was new to the participants, who were used to making decisions almost mechanically, usually under pressure to produce results immediately and without further questioning. Already during the first meeting, the participants recognized that they did not really know each others' functions and that they had many stereotypes about their obligations and possibilities.

The participants reviewed the reality of each office in terms of staff versus load of work, as well as the difficulties each office encountered in dealing with the academic side of the university, which they had to serve. It became evident to all that many of their stories demonized the clients of the offices without addressing the real problems. The managers began to wonder if there were not other ways to approach their work.

The first benefit of the Care Group meetings was familiarity with one another as colleagues and not as rivals whose slow performance made one's own office look bad. Many issues of poor coordination of services— for instance, the intricate and bureaucratic processes for the simple act of buying a chair—made the managers aware of the need for better communication, shared information, and task coordination. Empowerment was key to people who heretofore had worked under an authoritarian model with a submissive and pleasing attitude, and creativity was not a word in their vocabulary.

One manager, Luis, initially participated in the Care Group because he felt that it was to his advantage to be seen there. His boss was part of the project, and, apart from that, a certain status came with being part of the new enterprise. Apart from this, he considered it a waste of time: Of course, all the procedures in his office, which he had run for years, were under control. Therefore, he was shocked to discover that his office, as others saw it, slowed down the rhythm of all the internal offices he served.

His first reaction was to place the blame elsewhere. "My providers are never on time." "The auditing department is too slow." "The faculties are always changing their mind." However, when the group began using the Ladder of Feedback consistently in their meetings, he and his colleagues came to understand the benefits of proper and respectful feedback. Getting to know the functions, limitations, and problems of each office made it plain that there were misperceptions about them. The group became an articulate working team. They shared concerns, they brought new ideas to the table, and they allowed themselves to be creative.

When the idea of action projects was introduced, the whole group started enthusiastically on the process. Each

Cultures are made through:	
Ideals	The hopes, visions, and values explicitly referenced that drive new behavior
Leaders	The individuals who inspire, support, model, and mentor new behaviors, ideals, and tools
Tools	The explicit strategies, concepts and protocols that inspire, guide, and support new actions
Actions	The acts themselves that encourage and, moreover, evidence new behaviors, perceptions, beliefs, and values

head of department shared his dreams and mysteries, planned new actions, and received feedback and support from colleagues. Managers from the Care Group began to apply the Compass of Inquiry and different tools for communication. Luis shared with the people in his office not only his general reflections and action project but also other ideas and tools. Subsequently, a collective action project in Luis's office bore fruit. From the initial fifteen steps needed to serve a client, the office team reduced the procedure to four steps. Moreover, Luis soon reached agreements with other offices involved in the process in order to make it more agile and efficient. Beyond these specific accomplishments, a new energy and enthusiasm for work prevailed in Luis's office. People began to test taken-for-granted ways of operating, speak their minds, and work with their colleagues toward new modes of operation.

A Culture Clash

The Understanding for Organizations project at La Universidad Jorge Tadeo Lozano exemplifies how one can begin with the transformation of particular persons placed in different corners of the organization. Their gains in individual understanding and beliefs about the organization and how it can work seeded a wider process of cultural change. Participation in the Generative Life, Symbolic Conduct, and Care Groups, active work on their modes of communication, and attention to the Compass provided new insights, ideals and techniques for each of these high-level managers. In their own office settings, they became leaders of influence, sharing the ideals and insights and applying the tools. When supported by the organizational leaders, their models and lessons influenced others throughout La Tadeo.

This was Understanding for Organizations at its best. Inevitably, the pattern of development was more modest with many other individuals and offices. However, the greatest challenge occurred in the spring of the third year, when the initiative had settled down, gained new participants, and was approaching maturity. An unexpected decision by Colombia's Constitutional Court regarding labor contracts with adjunct professors, produced a significant overnight increase in the costs involved in operated higher educational institutions like La Tadeo. In reaction, the board of trustees at La Tadeo looked for ways to compensate and cut costs. They solicited an assessment of the processes, efficiency, and cost structure of the administrative offices from a firm that specialized in *reengineering,* a process that emphasizes streamlining and simplification of processes within an organization. This decision and consequent ones about reengineering contrasted sharply with the Understanding for Organizations project.

The initial assessment caused much anxiety amongst all of the administrative staff at La Tadeo—especially because the administrators received little warning. A group from the outside consulting team appeared in managers' offices, requesting certain pieces of information on operations. One office head even refused to admit them, on the grounds that he had no official notification of their status. But what was happening soon became clear to all. Many administrators recognized the danger of losing their jobs. The black business suits many of the consultants wore led many managers to nickname them *"the men in black,"* after the alien immigration duo in the movie of the same name.

The Rector, recognizing the fear in his community, did what he could to put a positive spin on the situation, stating that this would be an opportunity for recommendations from the consulting group to strengthen the effectiveness of the administration, without necessarily laying anyone off. However, he too worried about the impact, not only on morale but also on the livelihoods of many individuals he had come to know well and support over some time.

Soon the consultants presented their findings to the board. They identified many process inefficiencies and offered a guarantee that further recommendations based on a thorough assessment and analysis would amply cover the University's investment in the consultation. With their fiscal concerns in mind, the Board hired the consulting firm. Two weeks later, the consultants arrived at La Tadeo. A couple of months after they submitted their final report, some eighty administrators were dismissed.

From the first visit through the prolonged assessment procedures and the eventual firings, many of the once-enthusiastic participants in Understanding for Organizations began to lose motivation and participated less actively. A few even dropped out entirely. Many stated outright that they had once seen the activities as ways of supporting internal change and development, fueled by the commitment and ingenuity of the community, but now they had a lack of confidence in the leadership of La Tadeo.

In general, the intervention of the reengineering group reversed the process of cultural change. People were disconcerted, bewildered by the conflicting messages sent by the two different programs, one initiated and promoted by the Rector based on human resource development, the other a cost-cutting initiative directed by the board focused on productivity. Administrators who had been motivated and steadfast in their work with Understanding for Organizations often fell back into old behaviors and mindsets, even when they continued to go through the motions of participating. Indeed, regression to prior practices in the face of stress is a well-known psychological phenomenon. Many individuals quickly adopted defensive behaviors to safeguard their positions and place themselves at less risk. Corridor talk promptly returned as the main communication system, with gossip and speculation the order of the day. Many action projects were dropped. People deserted the project's meetings to concentrate on their routine work and demonstrate their efficiency. Lack of motivation and fear became common feelings.

This was indeed a setback. However, it is important to emphasize that many administrators kept the faith. They continued their action projects and their participation in other activities of Understanding for Organizations. The Rector and others high in the administration sustained their public support of the project. The researchers became counselors, their office a refuge for those who needed advice or simply needed to feel valued. After the wave of dismissals, La Tadeo researchers' roles gradually changed. Throughout the project, they were facilitators of manager's inquiry and model builders with Project Zero. Now they were in positions to institutionalize the project's ideas as part of the University's human resource development strategy. At the writing of this book, La Tadeo researchers have initiated a much-needed organizational learning project with their library system based on these ideas. The researchers continue to help this office and others implement approaches to building individual, office and organizational understanding.

Culture as a Long-Term Investment

The cases described in this chapter offer evidence that cultural change can occur through a self-empowered and gradual process, using explicit tools for developing new ways of perceiving, thinking, and acting, supported by resonant forms of leadership, and inspired by a shared set of ideals.

When this initiative commenced at La Tadeo, hopes for innovation and some first steps mingled with entrenched beliefs and practices, the legacy of times when the university was much smaller and functioned in a simpler and more traditional way. The changes began with individuals' growing awareness of the cultural elements that seemed troublesome in such areas as communication, leadership, and action. The participating managers became key agents of change, building new understandings in themselves and others through action. Felipe felt supported and empowered through his interaction with other managers in the Generative Life Group, eventually deciding to engage his staff in a process of getting to know each other better and devising new ways to manage the department. Claudia began an action project that guided her and her office in rethinking how things worked. Finally, Luis and his colleagues demonstrated how a group of individuals might change their outlook and practices over several offices, a scale that looked toward the whole organization.

However, the reengineering project's arrival late in Understanding for Organizations lifespan demonstrated how fragile such gains can be. Sustained championship from top leadership is crucial to establishing and stabilizing a new culture. The Board's decision to initiate a reengineering process sent messages very different from those signaled by the Rector through his support of the Understanding for Organizations project. Whereas Understanding for Organizations had placed humanistic ideals first in order of attention, while striving for operational and productive gains, the reengineering process inverted this order of priority. Its tools were not, by and large, tools for the staff of La Tadeo to use but for the consultants to use. Ideals, leaders, tools, actions— cultures can be made and unmade by the same forces.

Fortunately, the culture of understanding we sought was not wholly unmade. Matters have improved since the reengineering program. Still, we worry about the priorities of reengineering in contrast with Understanding for Organizations. It would be naïve to suggest that reengineering does not address problems worth solving. Certainly it does, and quickly. At the same time, we believe that organizational development should foster a long-term vibrant culture of commitment, energy, and participation. The choreography required to mix and meld abrupt adjustments introduced from outside with a sustained process of building from within is tricky, to say the least. What the outcome will be at La Tadeo remains to be seen. But at least this can be said: Many members of the La Tadeo community are working hard and thoughtfully to continue a pattern of growth.

Reflection

What cultural changes do you see your organization needing?

Is communication across groups or offices a major barrier to more effective and happier work in your organization? In what ways yes, in what ways no?

What kind of cultural shift would you like to see?

Have you encountered a culture clash in your organization, where different groups were promoting practices and attitudes that conflicted? What happened and why?

Action

Initiate a group to reflect on a cultural issue that seems relevant to transformation in your organization.

Give a survey to six departments to find out if they know what their neighbors do.

Consider your role from a top-down and bottom-up perspective.

When and where you are in a leadership position, think what you can do top-down to establish a positive culture—and do it! When and where you are one among several, think what you can do bottom-up, through setting an example, making suggestions, and so on—and do it!

8. Understanding for Organizations

Markers of Progress

The driving concept behind the action-research collaboration between La Tadeo managers and Harvard researchers was understanding—not just academic understanding but understanding in action. If an organization were to value understanding in action and become a place that could teach and learn for understanding, what would it look like? What would people be doing?

The focus on action was important. Neither managers nor researchers desired an organization that simply espoused ideals of reflection. The Rector did not want the managers in the community to act in impulsive and routine ways. He held forth a vision of members of the managerial community engaging in emphatically thoughtful actions and developing the know-how to improve their strategies, a vision of greater respect for one another and deeper collaborations. He looked toward each individual contributing more to the larger mission of La Tadeo.

In keeping with this vision, Understanding for Organizations yielded many real and important results for the university. Highlights from formal (surveys, interviews, and observations) and informal (stories, interactions, and participant-based anecdotes) data collection and analyses include:

- Insights on the part of managers about problems and opportunities in the culture, structure, procedures, and human relations at La Tadeo.
- Changes in the way managers talked with one another, adopting more constructive and supportive roles in the development of ideas, processes, and products.
- More personal and humane conversation concerning the emotional and psychological well-being of each other.
- Better community through interactions of sharing, caring, collegial support, and meaningful inquiry.
- The development of modeling, mentoring, and leadership practices, foregrounding respectful and constructive attention to group members, communication patterns, the cultivation of community, and the value of shared group inquiry.
- The impact of tools and support structures that fostered planning and action through articulation of strategies, allocation of time, and person-to-person support.
- The emphasis on practical strategies and practical action, which created a means for directly attending to shared concerns and issues of work.
- A more hopeful and proactive mindset.
- A number of concrete benefits concerning efficiency and quality of service emanating from the many action projects undertaken.

With these markers of progress in view, it's worth summing up the successes, shortcomings, and lessons learned in another way. We review the project through the four themes introduced in the first chapter, examining how well the project (1) bridged the idea-action gap, (2) created a culture of understanding in the organization, (3) integrated work and learning, and (4) established structural supports for the process. The treatment of each theme includes a brief account of what happened, an assessment of how well it went, and reflections on what might be done differently were it to be done again.

Bridging the Idea-Action Gap

Understanding in action by definition addresses the inherent challenges of moving people from just thinking and talking into cycles of reflection and action. La Tadeo managers often confessed that their organization was a place where people talked about problems and solutions but seldom did much. Innovation was rarely encountered, not expected, and sometimes even punished. At the project's inception, managers and researchers alike suspected that bridging the idea-action gap would be a major challenge. However, it was clear to all involved that learning for understanding had to take place through thoughtful action. True understanding at La Tadeo could emerge only through managers behaving differently, both individually and collectively.

The project researchers crafted several general strategies to help managers to bridge the idea-action gap. They created environments and expectations for action. They enrolled highly-placed administrators as public supporters and models. And they designed action-friendly frameworks and tools. Each of these strategies invites a few words on what was done and how well it worked, after which several comments appear about what might have been done differently to better bridge the idea-action gap.

Action Environments and Expectations

The stories throughout this book show managers collaboratively thinking and doing. From the outset, researchers knew that such concerted action would not occur just through sending interested managers to three-day workshops or asking them to read books. La Tadeo needed spaces and places for managers to reflect and act safely. Thus, the project included weekly meetings during which groups of managers came together to analyze the context of La Tadeo through the lenses of care, the generative life, and symbolic conduct, create action projects, and form Encuentros. These were social environments where meaningful action and practical inquiry were expected. Managers knew that to be a participant meant reflecting, experimenting, and giving and receiving feedback.

Not only did researchers, top managers and peers remind participants of this principle, it also received reinforcement through the formats and tools employed. The format of action projects required participants to meet with others, report their progress, share their puzzles, and give each other feedback. To ensure clear expectations, researchers often met with managers during the week to give them feedback. The larger meetings revealed to all who was acting and who was not. The Compass of Inquiry tool promoted both reflection and action as managers created their dreams and mysteries, then moved on to actions and evidence, repeating the spiral as necessary.

Top Managers as Public Supporters and Models

Public support and modeling by the organizational leaders was a second vital element in helping managers to bridge the idea-action gap. Throughout the project, the Rector and the Vice-Rector for Management and Finances allocated the money, created and protected the Friday meeting ritual, and attended meetings on a semi-regular basis. When spirits flagged, they reminded participants of the vision and the progress that had been made. All of these symbolic acts were essential for keeping the project alive and on track.

Several other higher-level managers also contributed by modeling the project's ideas in action. They created action projects along with their subordinates, and they spoke frankly in public about the personal and professional changes they had undergone. They used many of the tools and language explicitly, so other managers throughout the organization could see their utility. Of course, not everyone was on their best behavior all the time. Nonetheless, their contribution was central in bridging the idea-action gap with their managers.

Action-Friendly Frameworks and Tools

Throughout the project, the researchers strove to create concepts that could best bridge the idea-action gap with managers. The researchers simplified or avoided frameworks that involved many steps and contained cumbersome language. Thus, tools like the Ladder of Feedback and the Compass of Inquiry included only a few key ideas and terms. Managers reported that such frameworks were clear, used intuitive language, and were easy to recall in the midst of action.

Bridging the Idea-Action Gap

Helping managers move ideas into action was accomplished through strategies of:

- Action environments and expectations.
- Top managers as public supporters and models.
- Action-friendly frameworks and tools.

If We Were to Do It Again...

Introduction of action projects from the beginning of the initiative.

More work with high-level managers around symbolic conduct and its implications for supporting and sustaining the initiative.

More simple streamlined tools from the beginning.

These three areas saw many advances in the course of the project that helped managers to bridge the idea-action gap. However, challenges persisted at almost every turn. As noted in chapter 2, the initial work through the lens groups produced a great deal of worthwhile reflection but limited action. This led to the introduction of action projects within the lens groups. Were we to undertake such a project again, we would certainly include action projects as a beginning tool.

Although modeling by top management was key, it also occasionally backfired. High administrators fell under intense scrutiny by others in the organization. When a high administrator lost his or her temper, made a decision to fire someone, did not solicit feedback from others, appeared to be acting clandestinely, or seemed to be backing a controversial policy, this fostered cynicism. Comments like, "They really don't support these ideas," "How can they talk of understanding?" or "They aren't serious about change" frequently followed such natural missteps.

To deal with this better, researchers tried to meet regularly with high-level administrators, relay to them the sentiments of participants, reflect with them on their symbolic conduct, and improve their communication with the group. This proved somewhat successful. However, scheduling regular meetings with high administrators was difficult given their full plate of responsibilities. In hindsight, more focus in this area might have improved leaders' symbolic conduct and better supported all the managers in bridging the idea-action gap.

Another challenge was creating an array of simple action-oriented frameworks. This focus emerged as the project advanced through its middle and concluding stages. Thus, only a few of the many project concepts took on carefully developed action-friendly forms. The Ladder of Feedback and the Compass of Reflection were conspicuous successes, but many other concepts—for instance Corridor Feedback, Leadership through Questions, and Trust, remain to be refined into simpler, easier to use, and more memorable tools. In hindsight, an earlier focus on crafting actionable concepts might have resulted in more and higher quality tools toward bridging the idea-action gap.

Creating a Culture of Understanding

Besides bridging the idea-action gap, creating a culture of understanding-in-action was a second theme of the work at La Universidad Jorge Tadeo Lozano. The stories in earlier chapters illustrated four culture makers that helped to transform the administrative culture of La Tadeo: Ideals about understanding, the conduct of leaders, tools of inquiry, and actions along the way.

Public Ideals about Understanding in Action

Ideals lie at the core of change. Many organizational theorists, Peter Senge among them, have emphasized that people need more than just goals—sales targets, product development initiatives, new markets. They need a vision and a feel for why that vision is important. Perhaps an organization has a new mission to serve more clients, generate more business, or offer higher quality. If a change in thought and action is expected, people gain energy from the ideals that motivate and justify the fresh direction.

Those behind Understanding for Organizations sought to be explicit about its ideals. Through public speeches by high-level administrators, memos from the researchers, informational meetings and workshops, articles in the University magazine, and the weekly meetings, the vision of understanding in action gained presence. Values such as life-long learning, creativity, autonomy, democracy, generativity, human potential, and work as inquiry provide a foundation for an organization's shift toward understanding in action.

Leadership for Learning

The researchers worked closely with leaders at almost all levels on their leadership skills. Managers devoted many hours to refining their patterns of interaction—how they heard others' points of view, how they expressed their visions, and how they gave and received feedback. Through one-on-one researcher-manager meetings, researcher observations, workshops with small groups of managers, and groups of managers collaborating with each other in their offices, leadership patterns began to shift. Employees in the offices noted that people were speaking and responding differently, taking time to ask questions, to hear points of view, and to value what was good in each other's ideas. The common pattern of simply saying, "No, that will not work," dwindled. Managers and staff adopted more constructive practices, examining the roots of problems and brainstorming solutions. As the cases reported earlier showed, office leadership skills and their impact on office cultures were principal areas of success in the project.

Creating a Culture of Understanding

Attempts to shift the organizational culture towards cycles of action and reflection were done through:

- Public ideals about understanding in action.
- Leadership for learning.
- Tools for inquiry.
- Making progressive actions visible.

If We Were to Do It Again...

More emphatic and frequent framing of backsliding and similar problems as a normal part of the process.

A stable language for key ideals and tools early in the process.

Tools for Inquiry

Tools were another crucial resource for culture making at La Tadeo. As noted earlier, the researchers designed the form of these tools to bridge the idea-action gap. However, the content of the tools spoke directly to culture. For instance, the Compass of Inquiry fostered thoughtful action and a proactive mindset. Communication checklists and corridor feedback reflection sheets built awareness of patterns of interaction that often were negative, but could become positive. Managers reflected on their practice, raised questions, wondered, and experimented with new techniques and gathered feedback from others.

Making Progressive Actions Visible

Perhaps more than anything else, what people actually do in organizational settings establishes the culture, both through the direct impact their actions have and through their actions read as symbolic conduct. Accordingly, the researchers sought to make progressive actions visible. The many events during which participants shared their progress helped to sustain participants' interest and fuel further effort. Such events allowed managers within and outside of the project see and learn more about what was happening. The project established quarterly fairs during which managers shared posters of their action projects. Graduations were held, with the Rector and Harvard researchers giving "diplomas" to project participants. The public celebration of managers' actions played a vital symbolic and reinforcing role in shifting the culture of management towards understanding in action.

Though these areas show good progress, many difficulties stood in the way of establishing a culture of understanding in action. For example, the previous section noted that leader figures' actions fell under close scrutiny. The same was true for the middle managers. Occasional backsliding into old practices—a perfectly normal phenomenon—often provoked discouragement and cynicism. While the researchers persistently worked with managers around sharpening their awareness and skills, it would probably have helped to frame expectations more frequently and emphatically, so that occasional backsliding and other awkward episodes were seen as normal parts of the process rather than as signs of faltering or failure.

Another such challenge involved establishing and communicating a consistent set of project ideals through a consistent language. This was a developmental project. As noted before, the managers and researchers were "sailing the boat as we built it." The language changed from year to year. Early on, managers talked publicly about the importance of *generative topics* and *understanding goals.* A year later, the language evolved to refer to *dreams* and *mysteries.* Every month, the researchers were creating, trying out, and refining concepts and labels with the managers. Though the language of ideals and tools stabilized toward the end of the project, such a dynamic beginning created problems along the way. Some managers expressed confusion about the name of a tool, its steps or why an organization for understanding was important to La Tadeo. Although there was little choice for this project, further work in the same style could benefit from a more stable language of ideals and tools from the first, even as further innovations would undoubtedly emerge.

Integrating Work and Learning

Understanding for Organizations sought to make learning a part of work rather than something separate from it. This commitment involved integrating strategies that fostered learning into the managers' work practices. One way to reflect on the approach and results recognizes three learning time zones: learning in the moment, learning day-by-day, and learning through long-term initiatives.

Learning in the Moment

Many features of the project encouraged the managers to integrate learning into their work moment-to-moment. An interaction with a colleague, a memo in the making, or a brainstorm session all afforded managers moments to learn. Learning in the moment often involved the leadership and communication tools. For example, the Ladder of Feedback fostered learning in the moment, both by the giver and the receiver, through promoting clarification and the valuing of positive features, as well as through the suggestions for improvement. The leadership tools did likewise, introducing protocols that cultivated critical and creative thinking, and thus learning, during meetings and other interactions. Every day provided a wealth of moments for learning in the midst of action.

Learning Day by Day

The managers also engaged in daily or weekly strategies that integrated learning into their work. Action project groups met one or more times a week to share progress and give feedback. Many Friday mornings, the full group of participants gathered to reflect on progress and plan actions. A few managers began to car-pool to work to discuss and reflect on how their offices were doing. Such formal and informal strategies, often supported by protocols for conversation and feedback, helped managers learn day-by-day.

Learning through Long-term Initiatives

Finally, managers integrated learning into their work through longer term planning and reflective structures. Action projects organized by the Compass of Inquiry, with its dreams, mysteries, actions and evidence, guided managers' learning over many months. The Compass also coordinated group projects in some offices for the entire year. As mentioned earlier, quarterly meetings allowed managers to share large-scale progress, reflect, and gather feedback.

Many of the stories presented in earlier chapters illustrated these three levels of integrating learning at

Integrating Work and Learning

Supporting strategies of understanding into the flow of organizational work was done through attending to the various learning time zones. This was guided through creating practices for and a balance among:

- Learning in the moment
- Learning day by day
- Learning through long-term initiatives

If We Were to Do It Again

More attention to the substantial challenges of capturing fleeting moments of potential learning during the rapid flow of work.

Better tools for managers' handling of stress and resisting the relapses to earlier practices provoked by stress.

work. Probably the greatest challenge concerned the complexity and pace of managers' workflow. Every day, the managers faced a barrage of immediacies. It was not easy for a manager to recognize an opportunity to try out a new approach. Worse, crises and conflicts tended to evoke defensive emotions and behaviors. In such situations, managers usually and understandably reverted to well-established habits. Learning in the moment was a complicated endeavor, hinging upon a manager's ability to inhibit old habits, control emotional responses, and take risks. While many managers became adept at learning day-by-day and over long periods of time, almost all struggled with learning in the moment. In the future, understanding the complexities of learning in the moment and generating better strategies to assist managers in capturing the moment and avoiding regression in the face of stress are important directions to consider.

Establishing Structural Supports

Ideals, strategies, concepts and the like can only go so far in stimulating change. They easily evaporate in the face of organizational realities unless they are anchored in the very structure of organizational life. Throughout Understanding for Organizations, managers noted the need for a strong system of support—policies, established customs, written guidelines, and staff—to introduce and stabilize new ways of thinking and acting. Such structures help to create what many theorists call organizational memory. Through organizational memory, the organization can continue and expand an initiative even as individuals come and go. Let us review what was done around policies, customs, guidelines, and staff, concluding with an assessment of what could have been done better.

Official Policies

To encourage understanding in action, many managers and organizational leaders established official learning-orientated policies in their offices. At the top level, the Rector and financial Vice-Rector declared a policy that every Friday morning for two hours, mid-level managers would have time for activities related to Understanding for Organizations. Noting many successful action projects, a high level manager asked that subordinate office mission statements and yearly budgets incorporate dreams, mysteries, actions and evidence. Members of the La Tadeo administrative community have been continuing to strategize about infusing project ideas into further organizational policies such as hiring procedures, review process and personnel training, even as this book is written.

Established Customs

Many managers also established helpful rituals for themselves and those under them. As detailed in several cases discussed earlier, most managers soon established weekly meetings with their subordinates to discuss decisions, gather feedback, brainstorm solutions, and generally assess the progress of the office. Other managers scheduled lunches or coffee breaks with one another to touch base on work matters or deepen personal relationships. A few managers introduced tools such as the Ladder of Feedback as standard practice for the conduct of meetings. Some invited their colleagues into their offices to observe them in action and give feedback. Some organized regular retreats away from the organization toward relaxing, getting to know each other better, and reflecting on personal and office dreams for the upcoming year. Such informal customs not only helped to stabilize Understanding in Action, but offered evidence that La Tadeo had taken serious steps forward in its journey.

Printed Guidelines

Written artifacts to guide managers were also an important area of progress. For example, the managers created laminated inquiry cards small enough to be carried in a shirt pocket. The cards contained key project ideas and images such as the Compass of Inquiry and the Ladder of Feedback. The managers used these cards in meetings and showed them to other managers as a way of explaining the project. Other managers prepared memos and articles that offered their peers ideas about how to organize better their own inquiry and the inquiry process of others.

Support Staff

Many managers pointed to the important role the support staff played in developing understanding in action. As discussed in chapter 6, the structure here took the form of two internal personnel with positions dedicated to helping the managers as well as conducting research about the progress of the project. Further support came from several managers with a special interest who were encouraged to commit additional time helping others—what chapter 6 called the Internal Experts Group. External support came from contracting with the Harvard research and development team, members of which not only developed ideas and research plans, but participated in workshops and individual and small group working sessions.

These concrete structural elements certainly helped to put Understanding for Organizations in place and maintain its presence. However, as discussed in chapter 7, a change in the board of La Tadeo led to a reengineering project that shifted many managers' focus away from

---

Establishing Structural Supports

To support managers in developing understanding, the following types of structural supports were created:

- Official policies
- Established customs
- Printed guidelines
- Support staff

If We Were to Do It Again...

Secure the backing of the board of directors and other power groups, to protect the initiative better against the side-effects of changes introduced by parties who have little knowledge of it or commitment to it.

learning and understanding toward efficiency. The support structures continued throughout this period and sustained Understanding for Organizations, but with substantial drops in managers' commitment and momentum. Those managers that persisted reported feeling a loss of trust in the leadership. After the reengineering intervention ran its course, interest reawakened in some offices. However, in future initiatives, it would be wise to solidify the backing of a project like this one through the organization's board of directors and other relevant power groups.

Links to the Landscape

Understanding in organizations has its bright meadows and shadowy valleys. The experience at La Tadeo certainly shows that we should not expect a smooth process of change in such projects. Culture, work patterns, and organizational structures all are likely to be deeply entrenched, difficult to surface, resistant to change, and hard to stabilize after a process of change. As the authors reflect back, several features of Understanding for Organizations connect to challenges conspicuous in the landscape of literature on organizational development.

Relating Individual and Organizational Learning

A perennial question looms large among scholars and practitioners of organizational development: How do individual learning and organizational learning relate? For instance, to what degree does individual learning result in organizational learning? How can organizational learning yield individual learning? How can learning on both levels receive synergistic support?

Organizational psychologist Daniel Kim suggests that the link between individual and organizational learning lies in the development of shared mental models. He proposes that people have models of work, what it means, and how to do it. They interpret information and act according to those models. Organizational learning, according to Kim, depends on the degree to which everyone in the organization can change and improve their mental models toward a shared model. What may facilitate this process, as thinkers such as Conner, Kinicki, and Keats suggest, is the articulation of the models and their associated behaviors through the physical structures of the organization—files, procedural manuals, routines, traditions, and so on. Thus, learning would reside not only in each individual but also in the organization itself. Such organizational structures can be designed to coalesce individual models into a more collective vision—not a monolithic one but more in the character of a loosely shared script for action.

In this spirit, many steps taken by the managers at La Tadeo seemed to strengthen the link between individual learning and organizational learning. Tools were shared, adopted, and applied widely. The Compass of Inquiry became a point of reference for individual as well as collective action. The facilitators often communicated across groups, cross-pollinating ideas and stimulating mutual support.

Institutionalizing Learning

The literature on organizational learning consistently identifies it as a cornerstone of competitiveness. Such authors as Arie de Geuss and Lank and Lank argue that, without organizational learning, organizations will sink out of sight in the turbulent waters of today's quickly changing business environment. One way to ensure competitiveness is to institutionalize successful learning practices, ensuring that the organization always learns. As the organizational psychologist Mary Crossan and her colleagues put it:

The process of institutionalizing sets organizational learning apart from individual or ad hoc group learning. The underlying assumption is that organizations are more than simply a collection of individuals; organizational learning is different from the simple sum of the learning of its members. Although individuals may come and go, what they have learned as individuals or in groups does not necessarily leave with them. Some learning is embedded in the systems, structures, strategy, routines, prescribed practices of the organization, and investments in information systems and infrastructure.

While there are clear connections to the link between individual and organizational learning discussed above, Crossan and her colleagues place their primary emphasis on institutionalization of learning. Indeed, at least two kinds of learning are worth emphasizing. On one hand, there is learning that allows for continuous improvement of existing processes and products. On the other hand, there is learning that fundamentally redirects actions towards new processes and products. Institutionalization of learning in an organization should allow for both.

Evidence from La Tadeo argues that some project strategies attempted to institutionalize these two types of learning. The Compass of Inquiry along with communication tools and leadership strategies sometimes led managers to refine their existing practices and sometimes to craft very different ways of acting in their offices. Likewise, action projects allowed either for improving on current processes and products or striking out in new directions.

To Manage or To Learn?

Traditionally, managers view learning as an activity outside of the work environment—such as reading a book or going to a seminar. However, many authors today ask managers to become life-long learners, constantly developing through their daily performance. To paraphrase Joseph Raelin, a leading expert on work-based learning, there are three critical elements of the process:

- Managers learn in the midst of action and by being dedicated to the task at hand.
- Managers see knowledge creation and utilization as collective activities wherein learning becomes everyone's job.
- Managers demonstrate a learning-to-learn aptitude, which frees them to question underlying assumptions of practice.

Raelin, in alignment with Honey and Mumford's Learning Cycle, challenges managers to be activists, theorists, pragmatists and reflectors. And a major challenge it is! Most managers have little time. The need for actions and results often outweighs the need for reflection and theorizing. What little time managers do spend in meetings with others reflecting or theorizing may be poorly organized and feel like a complete waste of time.

As mentioned earlier, the researchers for Understanding for Organizations attempted to circumvent these problems by creating positive orderly learning experiences in the context of work. They designed protocols that helped individuals frame and design their learning within the work flow. Thus, Understanding for Organizations appears to have extended notions of work-based learning in the literature beyond the traditional action science or action learning interventions by building valuable learning directly into the everyday and necessary processes of organizational life.

The Sum of It All

While there continues to be abundant room for improvement, the varied fruits of this cross-cultural collaboration include the ideals, protocols, tools, and practices that support individual and organizational understanding in action. Many managers at La Tadeo continue to use these resources and continue to perceive, think and act in more humane and effective ways. The Rector's vision for La Tadeo to be a constructive culture of human development has taken some impressive initial steps forward through a community of administrators more aware of their dreams, articulate about their mysteries, assertive in their actions, and concerned with concrete evidence of progress. In such ways as these, the administrative community of La Universidad de Bogotá Jorge Tadeo Lozano advanced toward an understanding organization. They offer themselves as a inspiring example of how we all can surmount challenges in the quest for greater understanding in action.

Reflection

Is your organization already one that displays understanding in action? In what ways yes, in what ways no? Make a list of the ways. Write down specifics—specific people, events, processes, what you see and feel.

Is understanding in action something you would like to see more of in your organization? What would be the benefits? What would be the risks?

How could your organization move towards understanding in action? Who would be doing what? What are some of the possible leverage points (people, groups, offices, forums)?

What in particular could *you* do to move things forward?

Action

Raise the idea of understanding in action with friends and colleagues within your community. Tell them what you think. Ask them what they think.

Choose one or two modest areas within your circle of influence where you might move things forward. Recruit friends and colleagues. Strive for small but significant changes. Use some of the tools in this book.

After gaining some experience, try to capture the interest of people in positions of power and influence them toward a major initiative.

End Notes

1. Understanding in Action

An Expedition to the Chemistry Department

To learn more about Harvard Project Zero, see the website
http://pzweb.harvard.edu. Also an informative overview
can be found in *Harvard Graduate School of Education Alumni
Bulletin*, Dec 1994, 39(1).

A Commitment to Understanding

A comprehensive explanation of the Teaching for Under-
standing framework can be found in the following sources:
Tina Blythe's (1997), *The Teaching for Understanding Guide*
(San Francisco, Jossey-Bass); Martha Stone Wiske's (1998),
Teaching for Understanding (San Francisco, Jossey Bass);
David N. Perkins & Christopher Unger's "Teaching and
Learning for Understanding" chapter in C. Reigeluth's (Ed.)
(1999), *Instructional Design Theories and Models: Volume II*
(Hillsdale, NJ, Erlbaum).

A History of Expeditions

The Botanical Expedition in Colombia was the first scientific
mission, sponsored by Spain during the years 1783 to 1792.
Its purpose was twofold: to contribute knowledge to a
Natural History which was being collected in Europe and
to find new economic opportunities for Spain. As a result,
one discovery was the quina, a product later highly used

in medicine in Europe. This expedition not only had scientific results but also great economical, political and social influence. It was the inspiration for the mission of the Universidad Jorge Tadeo Lozano.

Understanding in Action

David N. Perkins provides the case for a performanced-based conception of understanding in his "What is Understanding?" chapter in Martha Stone Wiske's (1999), *Teaching for Understanding: Linking Research with Practice* (San Francisco, Jossey Bass).

The Teaching for Understanding framework elements are thoroughly presented in Martha Stone Wiske's chapter "What is Teaching for Understanding?" in her (1998), *Teaching for Understanding: Linking Research with Practice* (San Francisco, Jossey Bass). Perkins and Unger, cited above, also describe these elements and how they function.

Theme 1: Bridging the Idea-Action Gap

The idea-action gap can also be read about in David N. Perkins & Daniel Wilson's (1999), "Bridging the Idea-Action Gap," in *Knowledge Directions: The Journal of the Institute for Knowledge Management*, Vol 1, p. 64-77. Also, see Jeffrey Pfeffer and Robert Sutton (2000), *The Knowing-Doing Gap: How Smart Companies Turn Knowledge into Action* (Boston, Harvard Business School Press).

Espoused theories and theories-in-use are oft studied phenomena that can be found throughout Chris Argyris & Donald Schön's (1996), *Organizational Learning II: Theory, Method, and Practice* (New York, Addison-Wesley).

Organizational immune system is a term used by Edgar Schein and can be found throughout his (1997), *Organizational Culture and Leadership* (San Francisco, Jossey-Bass).

Manfred Kets de Vries' therapeutic perspective is found it his (1995), Life and Death in the Executive Fast Lane: Essays

193

on Irrational Organizations and Their Leaders (San Francisco, Jossey Bass) and his (1994), Organizational Paradoxes: Clinical Approaches to Management (New York, Tavistock).

Theme 2: Culture Makers

A useful and general perspective on cultures of learning can be found in Edgar Schein, cited earlier. Tishman and colleagues offer a cultural approach to fostering thinking in classrooms, also broadly relevant to organizations, in Shari Tishman, David N. Perkins, & Eileen Jay's (1995), *The Thinking Classroom* (Boston, Allyn and Bacon).

Theme 3: Integrating Work and Learning

Peter Senge's five disciplines can be found in his (1990), *The Fifth Discipline: The Art and Practice of the Learning Organization* (New York, Doubleday/Currency).

For further perspectives on the importance of integrating learning at work, see the Center for Workforce Development's 1998 report, *The Teaching Firm: Where Productive Work and Learning Converge* (Newton, MA, Educational Development Center).

Learning in the moment is akin to terms such as "just in time" learning, "reflective learning" or "learning in action." An interesting review of such topics can be found in David Garvin's (2000), *Learning in Action* (Boston, Harvard Business School Press).

Theme 4: Structural Supports

James March has dedicated years of research to understanding entrenched organizational routines and the structural barriers to organizational learning. For further reading into this area, see his (1999), *The Pursuit of Organizational Intelligence* (Malden, MA, Blackwell Business).

The focus and sequence of these chapter emerged through six multi-day meetings among the researchers from La Tadeo and Harvard spread out over the final year of the project. In a surprisingly rich collaborative writing experience, chapters and the potential foci were drafted in pairs, discussed in the team, swapped and redrafted by other authors. As a result, all chapters have at least three contributing authors, and some chapters as many as five.

2. Cultivating Consciousness

A Weekend of Reflection

The formation of the lenses of care, generative life, and symbolic conduct was driven by asking the top level leaders of La Tadeo to name some fundamental challenges that they, and the organization, are facing. An interesting and unplanned result was the language used for the lenses also embodied core values and commitments that the leaders held. The potency of framing changes using languages of commitments can be further seen in Robert Kegan and Lisa Lahey's (2000), *How We Talk Can Change the Way We Work* (San Francisco, Jossey-Bass).

Roberto's Office

The variety of offices involved in the project included those in charge of contracts, legal services, sales, plant maintenance, procurement, accounting, publications, library, research services, audio-visual equipment, engineering, administration, and finances.

The Lens of Care

On the theme of care, see such sources as: Stuart Wells (1997), *From Sage to Artisan* (Palo Alto, CA, Davies-Black); Roger Dow (1997), *Turned On: Eight Vital Insights to Energize Your People, Customers, and Profits* (New York, Harper

Business); Russell L. Ackoff (1999), "Transformational Leadership," in *Strategy and Leadership*, 27(1), p. 20-30; Diane McFerrin Peters (1999), "Employee Centered," in *Executive Excellence*, 16(2), p. 8; Barbara A. Glanz (1999), "Caring Workplaces," in *Executive Excellence*, 16(1), p. 16; Jay Liebowitz (1998), "You Can Become a Transformational Leader," in *Supervision*, 59(8), p. 14-17; Arie de Geus (1997), *The Living Company: Habits for Survival in a Turbulent Business Environment* (Boston, Harvard Business School Press).

The Lens of Symbolic Conduct

The theme of symbolic conduct aligns with the "symbolic frame," one of four "organizational frames" found in Lee Bolman and Terrence Deal (1997), *Reframing Organizations: Artistry, Choice, and Leadership* (San Francisco, Jossey Bass Management Series).

The Lens of the Generative Life

For notions connected with the theme of the generative life, see: Lotte Bailyn, Joyce K Fletcher, and Deborah Kolb (1997), "Unexpected Connections: Considering Employees' Personal Lives Can Revitalize Your Business," *Sloan Management Review*, 38(4), p. 11-17; John D. Ford and Laurie W. Ford (1995), "The Role of Conversations in Producing Intentional Change in Organizations," *Academy of Management Review*, 20(3), p. 541-571; John A. Shtogren's (1999), *Skyhooks for Leadership: A New Framework that Brings Together Five Decades of Thought - from Maslow to Senge* (New York, Amacom); Abraham Maslow et al (1998), *Maslow on Management* (New York, Wiley).

The Work of the Lens Groups

Similar strategies of organizing group inquiry in the workplace can be found in Elizabeth Kasl, et al's (1997), "Teams as Learners: A Research-based Model of Learning," in *The Journal of Applied Behavioral Science, 33*(2), p. 227-246; Yrjö Engeström's (2001), "Expansive Learning at Work:

Toward an Activity Theoretical Reconceptualization," in *Journal of Education and Work, 14*(1), p. 133-156.

Manager as Maestro

The notion of leaders as teachers appears from time to time in the literature of management. For instances, see Chip Bell's (1996), *Managers as Mentors: Building Partnerships for Learning* (San Francisco, Berrett-Koehler).

Bottom Lines, Plural

Senge's comment on the natural order of results regarding the three bottom lines was from an October 1999 conference entitled "Core Course: Personal Mastery and Systems Thinking," held in Bedford, Massachusetts. It was hosted by the Society for Organizational Learning, Cambridge, Massachusetts. For other related bottom line concepts, see Edgar Schein's (1996), "Three Cultures of Management: The Key to Organizational Learning," in *Sloan Mangement Review, 38*(1), p. 9-18; Peter Senge's (1996), "Leading Learning Organizations," in *Executive Excellence, 13*(4), p. 10; Peter Senge's (1997), "Communities of Leaders and Learners," in *Harvard Business Review, 75*(5), p. 30-32.

Assessment Using the Bottom Lines

The broadening of bottom lines to include social commitments and values can be further explored in John Elkington (1997), *Cannibals with Forks: The Triple Bottom Line of 21st Century Business* (Capstone, Oxford).

From Awareness to Action

Another illuminating discussion of the barriers posed when integrating awareness into action is described in Ellen Langer's (1997), *The Power of Mindful Learning* (Reading, MA, Addison-Wesley).

3. Integrating Work and Learning

The Three Fridays

On the challenges of transfer of learning, see Gabriel Salomon & David N. Perkins (1989), "Rocky Roads to Transfer: Rethinking Mechanisms of a Neglected Phenomenon," in *Educational Psychologist, 24*(2), p. 113-142. Also see David N. Perkins & Gabriel Salomon (1998), "Teaching for Transfer," which appeared in *Educational Leadership, 46*(1), p. 22-32. Further insights can be found in S.M. Cormier, & J.D. Hagman's (1987), *Transfer of Learning: Contemporary Research and Applications* (New York, Academic Press).

Foundations for integrating learning into the flow of work can be read in Kurt Lewin's (1951), *Field Theory in Social Science* (New York, Harper & Row).

Nancy Dixon's view can be found in her (1999), *The Organizational Learning Cycle* (Aldershot, Hampshire, UK, Gower Press).

Donald Schön writes much on this matter in his (1983), *The Reflective Practitioner: How Professionals Think in Action* (London, Temple Smith).

Work as Inquiry

Work as inquiry has much in common with other group learning approaches in organizations. For instance, similar concepts can be found in Etienne Wenger, Richard McDermott, & William Snyder's (2002), *Cultivating Communities of Practice* (Boston, Harvard Business School Press).

A Language for Learning at Work

Regarding the original TfU language, see sources cited in chapter 1.

The language was developed to be resonant with the local culture of La Tadeo. The labels would not likely meet success in another context. Bear in mind that labels were developed with the Spanish language in mind.

Camilo's Learning at Work

The case of Camilo was documented through interviews and observations by a team researcher who worked closely with him and his office to support their process.

Action Projects

A superb compilation of like-minded research can be found in Peter Smith & Judy O'Neil's (2003), "A Review of Action Learning Literature 1994-2000: Part 1—Bibliography and Comments," in *Journal of Workplace Learning, 15*(2), p. 63-69.

Stages of Action Projects

Similar cycles and stages of group learning in organizations can be read in: Nancy Dixon (1999), *The Organizational Learning Cycle: How We Can Learn Collectively* (Brookfield, VT, Gower); Yrjö Engeström (2001), "Expansive Learning at Work: Toward an Activity Theoretical Reconceptualization," in *Journal of Education and Work, 14*(1), p. 133-156; David Kolb's (1984), *Experiential Learning: Experience as the Source of Learning and Development* (Englewood Cliffs, NJ, Prentice-Hall); Kurt Lewin's (1948), *Resolving Social Conflicts* (New York, Harper); Marlene Scardamalia's (2002), "Collective Cognitive Responsibility for the Advancement of Knowledge," in B. Smith (Ed.), *Liberal Education in the Knowledge Society* (Chicago, Open Court).

Findings about Integrating Learning and Work

Action-reflection practices: Annikki Jarvinen & Esa Poikela's (2001), "Modeling Reflective and Contextual Learning at Work," in *Journal of Workplace Learning, 13*(7/8), p. 282-289; Kent Siebert's (1999), "Tools for Cultivating On-the-job Learning Conditions," in *Organizational Dynamics* (Winter), p. 54-63.

Comments by Peter Senge were made in a 1999 seminar cited in the Bottom Lines section of Chapter 2.

4. Smart Cultures of Communication

Wednesday's Ritual

The power of leveraging organizational rituals to support learning can be read about in Mica Popper & Raanan Lipshitz's (1998), "Organizational learning mechanisms: A structural and cultural approach to organizational learning," in *The Journal of Applied Behavioral Science, 34*(2), p. 161-179.

Not Just Nice, But Smart

Some additional sources on communication in the organizational literature: Anne Donnellon (1996), *Team Talk: The Power of Language in Team Dynamics* (Boston, Harvard Business School Press); Paul Drew and John Heritage's (1993), *Talk at Work* (Cambridge, England, Cambridge University Press); Gail Fairhurst and Robert Sarr's (1996), *The Art of Framing* (San Fancisco, Jossey-Bass,); John D. Ford and Laurie W. Ford's (1995), "Role of Conversations in Producing Intentional Change in Organizations," in the *Academy of Management Review, 20*(3), p. 541-71.

Generative Conversations

Argyris and Schön on the importance of testing one's conceptions: *Organizational Learning II,* cited in chapter 1. A wealth of insights on generative conversations can be found in William Isaac's (1999), *Dialogue and the Art of Thinking Together: A Pioneering Approach to Communicating in Business and in Life* (New York: Currency).

The Ladder of Feedback

On the power of feedback in supporting workplace learning, see: Susan Ashford & Anne Tsui (1991), "Self-regulation for Managerial Effectiveness: The Role of Active Feedback Seeking," in *The Academy of Management Journal, 34*(4), p. 251-280; Amy Edmondson (1999), "Psychological

Safety and Learning Behavior in Work Teams," in *Administrative Science Quarterly, 44*(4), p. 350-383.

Healthy Corridor Talk

Supporting social psychological accounts of corridor talk can be found in Grant Michelson & Suchitra Mouly (2002), "'You Didn't Hear It from Us But . . .': Towards an Understanding of Rumour and Gossip in Organizations," in *Australian Journal of Management, 27*, p. 57-66. For evolutionary accounts of gossip see Robin Dunbar's (1996), *Grooming, Gossip, and the Evolution of Language* (Cambridge, MA, Harvard University Press).

The felt lack of safety in organizations and how it harms potential learning can be read about in Anita Tucker & Amy Edmondson (2003), "Why Hospitals Don't Learn from Failures: Organizational and Psychological Dynamics that Inhibit System Change," in *California Management Review, 45*(2), p. 55-71.

Lessons in Crafting Smarter Cultures

Further reading on the barriers for disclosure and self-disclosure can be found in: Erving Goffman's (1973), "On Face-work: An Analysis of Ritual Elements in Social Interaction," in Bennis et al's (Eds.), *Interpersonal Dynamics* (Homewood, IL, Dorsey); Edward Jones & Thane Pittman (1982), "Towards a General Theory of Strategic Self-presentation," in J. Suls (Ed.), *Psychological Perspectives on the Self* (Hillsdale, NJ, Lawrence Erlbaum).

5. Leadership for Learning

Margarita and Jesus

The approaches the authors took to work with leaders like Jesus and Margarita were built upon the insights from Chris Argyris' (1991), "Teaching Smart People How to Learn," in *Harvard Business Review, 69*(3), p. 99-109. Also see Chris

Argyris' (1993), "Education for leading-learning," in *Organizational Dynamics, 21*(3), p. 5-17.

Leading Across the Gap

For alternative conceptions of the challenges of leadership and action, see Max DePree's (1990), *Leadership is an Art* (New York, Dell Books); Max Depree's (1993), *Leadership Jazz* (New York, Dell Books); and John Gardner's (1993), *On Leadership* (New York, Free Press).

Leadership through Questions

Similar accounts of counter-intuitive leadership approaches can be read about in: Linda Hill (2000), "Leadership as Collective Genius," in Chowdhury, S. (Ed.) *Management 21C: Someday We'll All Manage This Way* (London, Financial Times/Prentice-Hall); Barbara Kellerman (2005), "How Bad Leadership Happens," in *Leader to Leader*, Winter 2005, p. 41-46; Rakesh Khurana (2002), *Searching for a Corporate Savior: The Irrational Quest for Charismatic CEOs* (Princeton, NJ, Princeton University Press); David Perkins (2003), *King Arthur's Round Table: How Collaborative Conversations Create Smart Organization* (Hoboken, NJ, John Wiley and Sons).

The Bermuda Triangle

The three vertices of the triangle—people, process, and product—were built based on interviews with La Tadeo managers regarding how they made decisions. These vertices are reflected in the literature that studies the conditions that enable individual and group performance. For further reading see J. Richard Hackman's (1990), *Groups That Work (and Those That Don't)* (San Francisco, Jossey-Bass); J. Richard Hackman (2002), *Leading Teams: Setting the Stage for Great Performances* (Boston, Harvard Business School Press).

Much of the content of this section is based on David Perkins's (2003), *King Arthur's Round Table: How Collaborative Conversations Create Smart Organizations* (New York, Wiley). For additional perspectives see Piotr Sztompka's (1999), *Trust: A Sociological Theory* (New York, Cambridge University Press); Francis Fukuyama's (1995), *Trust: Social Virtues and the Creation of Prosperity* (London, Hamish Hamilton).

For a further discussion of fundamental attribution error see L. Ross' (1997), "The Intuitive Psychologist and His Shortcomings" in L. Berkowitz (Ed.), *Advances in Experimental Social Psychology*, Vol. 10 (New York, Academic Press).

An interesting and recent overview of self-fulfilling prophecies in management settings can be read in Brain D. McNatt's (2000), "Ancient Pygmalion Joins Contemporary Management: A Meta-Analysis of the Result," in the *Journal of Applied Psychology, 85*(2), p. 314-322.

Lessons about Leadership for Learning

For a similar account of how manages learned to negotiate power, answers, pressure and distrust, see Linda Hill's (2003), *On Becoming a Manager: How New Managers Master the Strategies of Leadership* (Cambridge, Harvard Business School Press).

6. Supporting Ongoing Change and Growth

A Day in the Life

Throughout the project an emphasis was placed on storytelling—creating spaces and formats for managers to share their experiences, challenges and share ideas through stories. For additional readings on the power of stories in organizations, see: Steve Denning's (2000), *The Springboard:*

How Storytelling Ignites Action in Knowledge-Era Organizations (Boston, Butterworth-Heinemann); John Seely Brown, et al's (1989), "Situated Cognition and the Culture of Learning," in *Educational Researcher, 18*(1), p. 32-42; Walter Swap, et al's (2001), "Using Mentoring and Storytelling to Transfer Knowledge in the Workplace," in *Journal of Management Information Systems, 18*(1), p. 95-114.

The Architecture of an Initiative

The four organizational frames of Lee Bolman and Terrence Deal are found in their 1997 book, *Reframing Organizations: Artistry, Choice, and Leadership* (San Francisco, Jossey Bass Management Series).

As mentioned earlier, Edgar Schein's view of organizational culture is found in his 1997 book, *Organizational Culture and Leadership* (San Francisco, Jossey-Bass).

Key Groups and Roles

Since the conclusion of the project, David Perkins has spoken in various conferences about how these five groups mirrored what he calls the three important visionaries necessary for successful change: political visionaries (the leadership team), conceptual visionaries (the external team), and practical visionaries (the internal team and participants). For further reading, see David Perkins (2003), *King Arthur's Round Table: How Collaborative Conversations Create Smart Organizations* (New York, Wiley).

The Activities

Literature on structures for change place emphasis on making the change public and in a variety of ways. For additional reading, see Larry Hirschhorn's (2002), "Campaigning for Change," in *Harvard Business Review, 80*(7), p. 8-104.

General Principles and Practices for Building a Culture

The principles of social constructivism can be read in Berger & Luckmann (1967), *The Social Construction of Reality* (New York, Anchor). Also see Alcoff & Potter (1993), *Feminist Epistemologies* (New York, Routledge).

Fostering Wide Participation

See Richard Elmore's "Getting to Scale with Good Educational Practice" in *Harvard Educational Review,* 66(1), Spring 1996, p. 1-26.

"But I'm Just One Person..."

For powerful insights into how individuals or minorities can influence majorities, see Robert Bray et al (1982), "Social Influence by Group Members with Minority Opinions: A Comparison of Hollander and Moscovici," in *Journal of Personality & Psychology,* 43(1), p. 78-88.

7. Toward a Culture of Learning

The Waters of Culture

For a further discussion of tacit knowledge see Robert Sternberg and Joseph Horvath (1998), *Tacit Knowledge in Professional Practice: Researcher and Practitioner Perspectives* (Mahwah, NJ, Erlbaum).

Felipe's Office

In conversations, managers often referred to their "masks" as their public faces they felt they needed to show. For many, these masks were artificial faces that covered up their true feelings and protected them from harm. Managers reported that, throughout this project, they dropped their masks, showing themselves as real people with emotions, ambiguous thoughts, and vulnerabilities. Topics such as "face-work" and "self-presentation" have been studied and can read about in the classic book by Erving Goffman (1959), *The Presentation of Self in Everyday Life* (Garden City, NY, Doubleday).

Claudia's Department

A lesson from Claudia's office was how interpersonal tension was generated from lack of clarity in office roles, tasks and processes. For further discussion on how the nature of the task can enable better performance, see J. Richard Hackman and Greg Oldham (1980), *Work Redesign* (Reading, MA, Addison-Wesley).

Luis's Office

A key move that Luis also adopted in his office was a process called 360 degree feedback, in which performance of an individual is collaboratively evaluated from subordinates, peers and boss feedback. See Mark R. Edwards and Ann J. Ewen's (1996), *360 Degree Feedback: The Powerful New Model for Employee Assessment & Performance Improvement* (New York, AMACOM) for a more detailed about of this methodology.

A Culture Clash

For a cautionary view of reengineering, see John Micklethwait and Adrian Wooldridge's (1996), *The Witch Doctors* (New York, Random House).

This phenomenon is often referred to as "cognitive downshifting." A rich discussion of it can be found in Joseph Ledoux's (1996), *The Emotional Brain: The Mysterious Underpinnings of Emotional Life* (New York, Simon and Schuster).

Culture as a Long-Term Investment

The long-term influence an organizational culture has on its employee's can be read about in Monica Higgin's (2005),

Career Imprints: Creating Leaders Across an Industry (San Francisco: Jossey-Bass).

8. Understanding for Organizations

Markers of Progress

Researchers on the team presented these findings to the leaders and participants, as well as circulated versions of these findings throughout the university via the organization's monthly newsletters. Aside, the markers cluster around the notion of the three bottom lines outlined in Chapter 2.

Bridging the Idea-Action Gap

The importance of informal and indirect learning in social environments can be read about in Victoria Marsick's work: Marsick, V. (2003), "Invited Reaction: Informal Learning and the Transfer of Learning: How Managers Develop Proficiency," *Human Resource Development Quarterly, 14*(4), p. 389-395; Marsick, V., & Watkins, K. (2001), "Informal and Incidental Learning," *New Directions for Adult and Continuing Education, Spring*(89), 25-34.

Creating a Culture of Understanding

Peter Senge treats ideals through one of his five disciplines, Shared Vision in his 1990 book, *The Fifth Discipline* (New York, Doubleday/Currency).

Integrating Work and Learning

Further discussion on the routines, tools and triggers of learning in the workflow can be read in Daniel Wilson's (2004), "Embedding Learning Strategies in the Workplace," a September briefing for Learning Innovations Laboratory, Harvard Graduate School of Education: http://lila.pz.harvard.edu.

For more on organizational memory, see James P. Walsh & Gerardo Rivera Ungson (1991), "Organizational Memory," in *Academy of Management Review, 16*(1), p. 57-91.

Links to the Landscape

This connection between individual and organizational learning is discussed in Daniel Kim's "The Link between Individual and Organizational Learning" in *Sloan Management Review,* Fall 1993, p. 37-50. Also see Patricia Corner et al's (1994), "Integrating Organizational and Individual Information-processing Perspectives on Choice," in *Organization Science, 5*(3), p. 294-308.

For more on organizational learning as the cornerstone of competitiveness see: Alden Lank & Elizabeth Lank (1995), "Legitimizing the Gut Feel: The Role of Intuition in Business," in *Journal of Managerial Psychology, 10*(5), p. 18-24; Arie de Gues (1997), *The Living Company* (Boston, Harvard Business School Press).

The quote from Mary Crossan and colleagues comes from: Mary Crossan et al (1999), "An Organizational Learning Framework: From Intuition to Institution," in *The Academy of Management Review, 24*(3), p. 522-537.

For more on the elements of work-based learning see Joseph A. Raelin's (2000), *Work-Based Learning: The New Frontier of Management Development* (Upper Saddle, NJ, Prentice-Hall) and Peter Honey & Alan Mumford's (1982), *The Manual of Learning Styles* (Peter Honey, Berkshire).